SEARCH, PONDER, AND PRAY

NEW ENGLAND

GUIDE FOR TRAVEL AND STUDY

Explore more Church History Sites in the Search, Ponder, Pray Series:

Historic Kirtland Guide for Travel and Study

Missouri Guide for Travel and Study

Illinois Guide for Travel and Study

CASEY PAUL GRIFFITHS & MARY JANE WOODGER

SEARCH, PONDER, AND PRAY

NEW ENGLAND

GUIDE FOR TRAVEL AND STUDY

ISBN 13: 978-1-4621-4350-4

Published by CFI, an imprint of Cedar Fort, Inc.
2373 W. 700 S., Suite 100, Springville, UT 84663
Distributed by Cedar Fort, Inc., www.cedarfort.com

Cover design by Courtney Proby

Printed in Colombia

10 9 8 7 6 5 4 3 2 1

Printed on acid-free paper

For my children,
Acacia, Joshua, Emmeline, and Grace.
Thank you for giving meaning to my journey.
–Casey

CONTENTS

ACKNOWLEDGMENTS

This series is the result of years of visits and study at the sacred sites of the Restoration. Over the years, dozens of missionaries assisted us in gaining access to the sites, sharing their insight, and their expertise they have gained from their service. First and foremost, we offer our gratitude to all of the missionaries of all ages and stages of life who have so graciously hosted us at the Church History Sites and allowed us to produce these guides. We offer our sincere thanks to Gary L. Boatright, who has acted as a liaison between us and the Church History Sites as we were doing our research.

A number of colleagues at Brigham Young University have also played a key role in helping us gain insights into the Church History Sites as well. Craig Manscil and Craig Ostler directed the BYU Travel Study program for several years, and the insights gained from extensive time at the sites with them and the wonderful students of the programs was invaluable in producing this book. Richard Bennett, Alex Baugh, and JB Haws also played a key role in funding site visits and contributing their expertise. Brent L. Top, Daniel K. Judd, and Scott C. Esplin all encouraged our research during their respective terms as the Deans of the College of Religious Education, and we appreciate their contributions and encouragement. We also wish to acknowledge the fund of the Religious Studies Center at BYU whose support made this volume possible. Finally, the wonderful editors at the BYU Faculty Publishing Service were a great help in preparing the final manuscripts.

We also appreciate the support and help of the wonderful contributors to Doctrine and Covenants Central, who generously allowed us to share materials written for their site in this volume. Scott Woodward played a key role in developing the site, and we appreciate John Welch and Kirk Magleby for reaching out to us to create such a wonderful resource to study Church History. Several staff members from Scripture Central, the parent site to Doctrine and Covenants Central accompanied us on trips to the sites and greatly assisted our work. These include Zander and Angel Sturgill, Benjamin Griffin, Taylor and Alexis Riley, Avery Kirk, and Daniel Smith. We are especially grateful for several student assistants who have been involved in varying degrees in the large task of selecting, transcribing, writing, and editing the material included in this manuscript. Isabel Tueller, London Brimhall, and Derek Charlton are surely some of the most cheerful, capable, dependable, and intelligent of assistants.

We also want to express our deep gratitude to Valerie Loveless of Cedar Fort Publishing & Media for her conception, vision, encouragement, expertise, and editing of our manuscript; she was indispensable in the creation of this series.

Finally, we express our gratitude to our families for all of their patience with the travel and research involved in producing this book. One of the great joys of our lives is taking our loved ones to these sacred places, and they are among our most cherished traveling companions. We hope that our work allows our readers to have special experiences at all of the sites, just as we have had!

INTRODUCTION: THE CRADLE OF THE RESTORATION

The Sacred Grove near the Joseph Smith Family Farm. Photo by Casey Paul Griffiths.

Every year, millions of pilgrims travel to Jerusalem, Mecca, India, and host of other locations around the globe. These travelers long to walk in the footsteps of sacred figures, see the lands of their scriptures, and maybe take home a bit of the sacred with them. We equate miracles of the past with lands distant from our own, but for Latter-day Saints holy sites are found all around us. One of the central teachings of the Book of Mormon is that Jesus Christ manifests Himself "unto all nations." For the Saints, sacred history is found not only in the ruins of ancient cities like Jerusalem but are also nestled among the modern towns and cities of the New World. Places like Palmyra, Fayette, and Harmony take their place alongside the holy sites of the Bible in the history of the Latter-day Saints. Through the events of the early Restoration the lush green forests of the eastern regions of North America take their place alongside the hills and valleys of Israel as the abode of angels and prophets. This beautiful landscape forms the cradle of the Restoration, the first places where God reached out to men and women in modern times to restore His Church to earth in the latter-days.

In making the pilgrimage to these sacred places we find connection and meaning to the stories of our own lives. If God knew the name of an obscure farm boy in a rustic village in upstate New York, He knows your name too. If Jesus Christ appeared to answer the questions of a fourteen-year-old seeking wisdom, He is aware of you and wants to answer your questions as well. If angels appeared to tutor, instruct, and guide a young frontier prophet, then angels can assist you in the daily struggles of your life. The strength and fortitude gained from the interventions of Heavenly beings can be passed on to us in the present. When we walk this holy ground we become a part of the sacred landscape, and the stories that took place in the cradle of the Restoration and find new life in our discipleship.

Why We Wrote This Book

This book is part of a series of guides designed to enhance your visit to the Church History sites. This volume focuses on the earliest sites of the Restoration, beginning with the birthplace of the Prophet Joseph Smith in Sharon, Vermont, and continuing through the various places he lived during his prophetic career. The New England states of Vermont, New York, and Pennsylvania were where the Prophet lived during his formative years with his family, first fell in love with his wife, Emma, and began the marvelous work of the Restoration. It has been our privilege to visit these sites on many occasions and feel the sense of the sacred in these beautiful locations.

However, any site can become just another stop on the road without a knowledge of the history that took place there. Many sites have visitor centers staffed by helpful missionaries who can assist you in knowing the story that makes the place sacred. Many pilgrims enlist the help of a guide during the travels through the lands of the early Restoration. On occasion, during our visits to the sites we have often seen families pull up to a site, wander a few moments, and then return to their car without fully knowing what makes the place they visited so special.

In the past there were many site books available concerned with just helping you with finding directions to the site. However, with the advent of new technology, finding most Church history sites has become relatively simple. This has rapidly increased the number of people who seek out these sites on their own. Because of this, directions to the sites have been placed in this book only when they are absolutely necessary. Instead, these books are designed to provide you with the background stories behind the sites. Whenever possible we have drawn from first-hand accounts produced by those who lived on these properties and played their vital roles in the work of the Restoration. The intent behind these books is to enhance your visits to the sites by putting primary sources into your grasp, arranged site by site.

Another notable departure in these volumes is the scope we have chosen. Many guidebooks have chosen to list every site possible within a given area. This can be very useful, but usually limits the narrative of a site to just a few paragraphs because of the need to cover every site. Where other authors have chosen breadth over depth, we have chosen instead to focus on the primary sites in each region and provide a thorough account of the events that took place there from primary sources. This means that there might be other places worth visiting not covered in this book. Near Mendon, New York, for instance, is the baptismal site of Brigham Young, which is difficult to find but well worth visiting. You might want to consult with the local missionaries if you are interested in visiting more out of the way sites like this one. For our purposes here, we have chosen to focus on the primary sites in each region.

How to Use This Book

This book is arranged to give you the stories that took place at each of the sites, with special emphasis on the relationship of each location to the scriptures, particularly the Doctrine and Covenants. Chapters are arranged roughly chronologically, beginning with Sharon, Vermont, where Joseph

Smith's birthplace, and concluding with the Peter Whitmer Sr. Farm, the last place Joseph Smith lived in New England before moving first to Ohio and then to other places during his prophetic ministry. Other books in this series will cover Church history sites and their stories in Ohio, Missouri, Illinois, and other locations.

Each chapter begins with a few bullet points which overview the most significant events at each site, and the revelations received at these locations. The story of behind the site is organized around these events, with emphasis given to the times and places where revelations were received that became part of the scriptural canon. Many New England sites, such as the Smith Family Farm in Palmyra or the Grandin Press, are staffed by missionaries who can also help guide you through the sites. These books are not intended to take the place of the missionaries, whose testimonies and teachings you find to be an important part of each site visit. The missionaries at the sites will help you find the key locations and share brief stories with you. These books are designed to enhance the experience you will have with the missionaries by providing you with the primary sources and cutting-edge scholarship behind each of the locations.

At other sites, such as Alvin Smith's headstone or the Martin Harris farm, missionaries are not available. These sites can be more difficult to locate. Information about these sites can be harder to find, so we have included photographs and more specific directions to find these sites. At these locations the information in this book will help you to act as your own tour guide, or serve as a guide to others. Sites without visitor centers or missionaries are often overlooked but can provide an array of edifying experiences if visitors are provided with the right information to enhance their visit.

In each chapter a series of mini-devotionals are embedded into the text to deepen your experience at each of the sites, using questions provided to guide your reflection on the site you visit or can be used to teach your friends and loved ones visiting the sites with you. At most locations you will visit, areas are provided where visitors can take a few moments for reflection. The devotionals provided point out some of the most important principles learned by the early Saints at this location. Taking a little time to reflect and review the events and personalities associated with each site will bring deeper meaning to your time spent in these special places.

Finally, we would remind you that reverence invites revelation. We would invite you to spend a few moments during your travels reading the revelations given by the Lord to the early Saints as they struggled to accomplish their work. As you do so, we feel you will become a part of the stories you are learning about. One of the great blessings of living in our time is that there is no end to the story of the Restoration for only those who pick up the sacred commandments and teachings given to the early Saints and make them a part of their own story. As you search, ponder, and pray in these holy places, we hope that your love for the Savior will increase, and your testimony of His work in the latter-days will continue to grow.

Casey Paul Griffiths
Mary Jane Woodger
General Editors

Significant events in this area:

- The Mayflower docked in Plymouth Bay, Massachusetts on December 16, 1620.
- Joseph Smith Sr. and Lucy Mack were married on January 24, 1796 in Tunbridge, Vermont.
- Brigham Young was born on June 1, 1801 in Whitingham, Vermont.
- The Prophet Joseph Smith was born on December 23, 1805 in Sharon, Vermont.
- Joseph Smith Jr. had surgery on his leg in 1813 Lebanon, New Hampshire.
- Wilford Woodruff went on a mission to the Fox Islands, Maine from 1837 to 1838.
- George A. Smith arranged the Smith Family Memorial in Topsfield, Massachusetts, in 1873.
- The Joseph Smith Birthplace Memorial in Sharon, Vermont was dedicated on December 23, 1905.
- The Smith Family Memorial in Topsfield, Massachusetts was renovated in 2019, and was rededicated in 2022.

THE BIRTHPLACE AND SEEDBED

Joseph Smith's Birthplace and Other Church History Sites in Vermont, New Hampshire, Massachusetts and Maine

The Joseph Smith monument at the Prophet's birthplace in Sharon, Vermont. Photo by Kenneth Mays.

Many members of The Church of Jesus Christ of Latter-day Saints consider Palmyra, New York, as the birthplace of the Restoration of the gospel. It is here that Joseph Smith, at the age of fifteen, went into a grove of trees and saw God the Father and his son Jesus Christ in a miraculous vision. However, when we think of the birthplace of the Restoration, we should not think of only New York. Joseph himself was born in Vermont in 1805, and many of the early Church leaders, including Brigham Young, Wilford Woodruff, Oliver Cowdery, and Hyrum Smith, were born in the surrounding New England states. More than two dozen other early General Authorities were native to the New England area. Many of the first latter-day converts accepted the gospel in New England, and many of these converts were the descendants of the area's first settlers.[1]

New England was one of the first areas to be established as a British colony when settlers crossed the Atlantic Ocean hoping to practice religion without government interference. When the *Mayflower* landed on the shores of Massachusetts, the seeds for the Restoration of the gospel of Christ were planted once more in the land of promise. From the revelations and visions given to Nephi in the Book of Mormon, we know that the establishment of the United States was of divine intention—to build a foundation for the Church of Jesus Christ to be restored to the earth (1 Nephi 13:12–15). The government that came from the legacy of these colonists would allow early members of The Church of Jesus Christ of Latter-day Saints to experience the blessings of religious freedom. It was this religious freedom that fostered the questions of a fifteen-year-old boy—questions that urged him to go into a grove of trees and seek knowledge about Christ's everlasting gospel. This boy would see God the Father and his son Jesus Christ in a miraculous vision in the grove of trees, and many years later, he would open the final dispensation of the gospel of Christ.

Because it is connected to many early Church members, the New England area has become a sojourn for many. As you explore and wander the roads of the monuments and farmlands of the early Saints—from the legacy of the Smith family to the Fox Islands of President Wilford Woodruff's mission in Maine—you will see that "New England . . . is the birthplace and seedbed of Mormonism."[2]

---

1 Keith W. Perkins et al., "New England Symposium: 1985 Introduction," in *Regional Studies in Latter-Day Saint Church History: The New England States*, ed. Donald Q. Cannon, Arnold K. Garr, Bruce A. Van Orden, and Brigham Young University (Provo, UT: Brigham Young University Religious Studies Center; Salt Lake City: Deseret Book, 2004), 10.

2 Perkins et al., "New England Symposium," 10.

Mayflower Replica, Plymouth Bay

The Mayflower II moored at Plymouth, Massachusetts.. Photo by Benjamin Griffin.

In many of Nephi's recorded visions, he saw events that would transpire in the latter days. In one vision, Nephi saw Christopher Columbus "discover" the American continent: "I looked and beheld a man among the Gentiles, who was separated from the seed of my brethren by the many waters . . . and he went forth upon the many waters, even unto the seed of my brethren, who were in the promised land" (1 Nephi 13:12). He also saw other Gentiles sailing across the sea, and he saw these people prosper and obtain the land for their inheritance (1 Nephi 13:14–15). These Book of Mormon prophecies may refer to any person led by the Spirit to the New World. The also hold special application for the Pilgrims, sailing across the sea on the *Mayflower* to a land where they were promised a blessing they had been deprived of: the freedom of religion. No matter whether they left England by choice or were driven away, the Pilgrims were determined to purify and reform the Church of England. They hoped to return to their home country one day and be welcomed back by those who would recognize and accept the work God wrought through them.[3]

Among the Pilgrim settlers were seven ancestors of the Prophet Joseph Smith: Edward Fuller, his wife, and their son, Samuel; John Tilley, his wife, and their daughter, Elizabeth; and John Howland, who married Elizabeth Tilley.[4]

As you look at the replica ship docked in the Plymouth Bay harbor, you can imagine the living conditions that these people had to endure as they journeyed across a dangerous ocean to a land that they knew little about and where they would start life over from scratch. Of the 102 passengers and 25 crewmembers that made it to America, all but 44 of these Pilgrims died within their first winter in this new land. Among the dead were Edward Fuller, John Tilley, and both of their wives.

Mini-Devotional—Trials of Faith

Imagine a scene aboard a cramped, wet, and sickness-filled boat. It is the year 1620, and you are one of the lucky few to have the opportunity to travel to the New World. A great storm is raging on the sea, and the crewmembers are struggling to keep the ship afloat. Despite these terrifying odds, you remain strong because of your faith in God. You have hope that this journey will be successful and bring you to a better life in a better land.

- What are some ways that faith has given you courage to overcome trials in your life?
- What are some ways that you can strengthen your faith in Heavenly Father and the Savior?

Fast forward to the winter of the following year. Forty-five of the original 102 passengers of the *Mayflower* have died, but you continue forward,

---

3 James R. Christianson, "Puritanism and Mormonism: Parallel Paths, Parting of Ways," in *Regional Studies in Latter-Day Saint Church History: The New England States*, ed. Donald Q. Cannon, Arnold K. Garr, Bruce A. Van Orden, and Brigham Young University (Provo, UT: Brigham Young University Religious Studies Center; Salt Lake City: Deseret Book, 2004), 42.

4 Craig J. Ostler, "Glimpses of Church History in New England: A Photo Essay," in *Regional Studies in Latter-Day Saint Church History, New England*, ed. Donald Q. Cannon and Brigham Young University (Provo, UT: Brigham Young University Department of Church History and Doctrine, 1988), 174.

building homes and shelters for not only your own company but the many of thousands of migrants that will join you in the coming years. As you settle into the New World, you remain faithful to your belief in God and to the mission you swore to fulfill. You are a city set on a hill, in open view of all the earth.[5] You will set an example for the rest of the world so that you can one day return to the Old World bearing the kingdom of God on your shoulders.[6]

- What are some blessings you have noticed in your life by having faith in Jesus Christ?

Thank your Father in Heaven for inspiring these brave men and women to help these brave men and women to help prepare the land for the Restoration of the gospel.. Elder Dieter F. Uchtdorf observed, "Often, all we see is the path directly ahead—we cannot see where the bends in the road will lead."[7] Trust that your Heavenly Father will lead you on the path towards your own eternal destiny.

The Smith Family Memorial Monument, Topsfield, Massachusetts

The Smith Family memorial monument in Topsfield, Massachusetts. Photo by Kenneth Mays.

When Latter-day Saints think of Church history sites of significance, Topsfield, Massachusetts, is probably not the first town they think of.

5 Christianson, "Puritanism and Mormonism," 43.
6 Christianson, "Puritanism and Mormonism," 42.
7 Dieter F. Uchtdorf, "Come and Belong," *Ensign*, May 2020, 104.

However, among the first residents of Massachusetts in or near the town of Topsfield were five generations of Joseph Smith's paternal progenitors. The Smith family was a prominent presence in Topsfield, starting with Robert Smith, who immigrated to Massachusetts from England, and his wife Mary French Smith.[8]

Robert Smith was fifteen years old in 1638 when he emigrated from England and arrived in Boston, Massachusetts, where he worked as an indentured servant and later as a tailor. When he later moved north to Ipswich, he met Mary French, a native of Boston. They married in 1656 before moving to Rowley, Massachusetts (later known as Boxford). The couple had ten children together, one of which was Samuel Smith I. Robert later settled the Smith homestead in Topsfield, where five generations of the Smith family would live for most of their lives.[9] Samuel became the executor of the homestead after Robert's death.

Of all the Smiths that lived in Topsfield, Samuel Smith I's son Samuel Smith II was the most distinguished. Samuel II served as a town clerk and as Topsfield's selectman and was a member of the Tea Committee, the Committee of Safety, and the Committee of Correspondence. Most notably, Samuel II represented Topsfield as a delegate to the Provincial Congress in 1775 and served as captain of the Topsfield militia.[10]

The youngest son of Samuel Smith II and his wife, Priscilla Gould Smith, was Asael Smith. Asael and his wife, Mary Duty Smith, moved from Topsfield to New Hampshire in 1772, where he would serve in the Revolutionary War. Asael, his wife, and their ten children returned to Topsfield in 1786, where their youngest child was born three years later. In 1791, Asael sold the Smith homestead and moved his family to Tunbridge, Vermont.

A deeply religious man, Asael Smith prophesied that something would come forth from his posterity to revolutionize the world. When word about the visions of his grandson Joseph Smith Jr. reached him, Asael stated "that he always knew that God was going to raise up some branch of his family to be a great benefit to mankind."[11] Apostle George A. Smith, cousin to Joseph

---

8 Alexander L. Baugh, "The Smith Family Memorial Monument in Topsfield, Massachusetts" *BYU Religious Education Review*, Fall 2021, 14.

9 Baugh, "Smith Family Memorial Monument," 18.

10 Baugh, "Smith Family Memorial Monument," 18.

11 Sydney Walker, "Topsfield: The Prequel to Joseph Smith's Story that Helped Lay the Groundwork for the Restoration," *Church News*, December 7, 2020.

Smith Jr., recorded: "My grandfather Asael fully believed in the Book of Mormon, which he read nearly through, although in his eighty-eighth year, without the aid of glasses." Unfortunately, because of Asael's weakened and aged condition, he was unable to be baptized and died shortly after this meeting in Potsdam, New York, in October 1830. However, his wife, Mary Duty Smith, joined the Saints in Kirtland, Ohio, in May 1836 along with her grandson Elias. Joseph Smith Jr. recorded, "She had not been baptized on account of Jesse Smith, her eldest son, who has always been an enemy of the work. . . . My grandfather, Asael Smith, long ago predicted that there would be a prophet raised up in his family, and my grandmother was fully satisfied that it was fulfilled in me."[12] Mary fell ill a few days after arriving in Kirtland and died on May 27, but she remained firm in the faith, despite not being baptized.[13]

In 1873, George A. Smith arranged for a memorial that would honor Samuel Smith I, Samuel Smith II, and their wives, who are said to be buried in the Pine Grove Cemetery, located by Topsfield's town center. Because the cemetery did not exist at the time of Robert and Mary French Smith's deaths, it is likely they were buried elsewhere, so their names were not included on the memorial. Asael Smith and his wife, Mary Duty Smith, are also not buried there since Asael died in Potsdam, New York, and Mary died in Kirtland, Ohio.[14] In 2019, the Church announced plans to clean and renovate the monument—this time commemorating all five generations of the Smith family that lived in Topsfield. The project was originally scheduled to be dedicated in June 2020, but the COVID-19 pandemic delayed the monument's construction, so the dedication was postponed. On September 25, 2020, the five stone sections commissioned and created for the monument were assembled and fitted on the site, thus completing the project. Dedication is set to take place in 2022, with hopes that the Acting President of the Quorum of the Twelve Apostles and great-great-grandson of Hyrum Smith, M. Russell Ballard, will attend and dedicate the site. This renovated monument will stand as a lasting tribute to the Smith family's incredible heritage.[15]

---

12 Joseph Smith, *History of the Church of Jesus Christ of Latter-day Saints*, ed. B. H. Roberts (Salt Lake City: Deseret Book, 1957), 2:442–43, in Ostler, "Glimpses of Church History," 183–84.

13 Ostler, "Glimpses of Church History," 183–84.

14 Baugh, "Smith Family Memorial Monument," 18.

15 Baugh, "Smith Family Memorial Monument," 18.

Mini-Devotional—Lessons from Ancestors

As you step through the cemetery and approach the Smith Family Memorial Monument, you may notice that its spire stands like a light on a hill. Think of all the members of the Smith family that called this area home and how their faith in God influenced the boy that would become the Prophet of the Restoration. Think about your own ancestors and the stories and lessons they can teach you as you sit on the stone benches within the monument boundaries.

- What ancestral stories have helped shape your faith?
- What are some ways you can learn about and serve your ancestors?

Pray and thank your Heavenly Father for your heritage, and pray for the spirit of Elijah to be with you, to inspire you to reach out to your ancestors and learn their stories and what they can offer you.

Home of Solomon Mack II and Solomon III, Gilsum, New Hampshire

Stone arch near Gilsum, New Hampshire. Photo by Kenneth Mays.

Vermont and Massachusetts are not the only New England states that played an important role in early Church history. Joseph Smith Jr.'s maternal ancestors are connected to the state of New Hampshire. Solomon Mack, Joseph's grandfather, moved from Lyme, Connecticut, and settled in the Marlowe, New Hampshire, area in 1761. He moved to Gilsum, New Hampshire, around 1773. Gilsum is where Solomon and his family would settle and live for most of the rest of their lives, despite still owning land in Marlowe.[16]

Lucy Mack Smith was born in Gilsum in a log cabin on July 8, 1775. The log cabin is located on the southeastern side of the Centennial Bond Cemetery in Gilsum, New Hampshire. It now stands as a private, fenced residence and is not open to the public. The maternal grandfather, uncle, and cousin of the Prophet Joseph Smith, all of whom were named Solomon, played vital roles in connecting the town of Gilsum to Latter-day Saint history.

Solomon Mack II, Joseph's uncle, built a second home in Gilsum in 1835, and it later served as the meeting place of the Gilsum branch's reorganization in 1849. Lucy Mack Smith wrote to her brother and his wife, Esther, to share the news of the coming forth of the Book of Mormon and the Restoration of the gospel. This letter planted the seeds of faith and bore fruit in the Mack family in Gilsum. According to historical records, Solomon II and his family were baptized and remained strong members of The Church of Jesus Christ of Latter-day Saints in their Gilsum branch. Solomon II's sons, Solomon III and Chilion, would serve as branch president and branch clerk, respectively.[17]

---

16 A. Gary Anderson, "The Mack Family and Marlow, New Hampshire," in *Regional Studies in Latter-Day Saint Church History: The New England States*, ed. Donald Q. Cannon, Arnold K. Garr, Bruce A. Van Orden, and Brigham Young University (Provo, UT: Brigham Young University Religious Studies Center; Salt Lake City: Deseret Book, 2004), 88.

17 Ostler, "Glimpses of Church History," 185.

The large headstone on the left marks the burial place of Solomon Mack, the father of Lucy Mack Smith.Photo by Kenneth Mays.

Mini-Devotional—Sharing the Gospel

Imagine the excitement that Lucy Mack Smith felt as she shared the news of the restored gospel with her family. She must have felt such joy when they were baptized and joined the Church. Also imagine the joy that her brother Solomon Mack II felt when he received the message and the blessings that he and his family received upon being baptized.

- Who are some people that you have shared or want to share the gospel with?
- Brainstorm different ways you can share the gospel of Jesus Christ and the love of God with these people.

Pray for inspiration and courage to share the gospel within your own family. Pray for Heavenly Father to bless and inspire the missionaries serving around the world to find those who have been waiting and preparing to receive the gospel of Jesus Christ.

Stephen Mack's Store, Tunbridge, Vermont

This structure, then a sawmill, was part of Stephen Mack's business. Photo by Kenneth Mays.

Lucy Mack Smith's early life could be described "by death and illnesses."[18] When she was three, her father, Solomon Mack, suffered from two separate falling accidents—the first from a tree and the second from a waterwheel. He left for Nova Scotia when Lucy was eight, and her mother, Lydia Gates Mack, suffered from a "severe fit of sickness" not long after.[19] Lydia ultimately left Lucy in the care of her older brother Stephen Mack. When Lucy was fourteen, her married sister, Lovisa Mack Tuttle, fell ill with consumption along with another sister, Lovina Mack, who was a year younger than Lovisa. For the next five years, both sisters would hover above the brink of death. And at age sixteen, Lucy would carry incapable Lovina, age twenty-nine, from chair to bed.[20]

18 Richard L. Bushman, "The Joseph Smith Family," in *Joseph Smith: Rough Rolling Stone*, ed. Alfred A. Knopf and Jed Woodworth, (New York, NY: Knopf Doubleday Publishing Group, 2005), 11.

19 Bushman, "Joseph Smith Family," 12.

20 Bushman, "Joseph Smith Family," 12.

This building in Tunbridge, Vermont was also part of the complex of businesses owned by Stephen Mack.. Photo by Angel Sturgill.

After Lovina and Lovisa's deaths, Stephen Mack invited depressed Lucy Mack to visit him in Tunbridge, Vermont.[21] It was during her visit to Tunbridge that Joseph Smith Sr. and Lucy met.[22] Stephen was a very prominent businessman in the town of Tunbridge; he owned a sawmill, gristmill, blacksmith shop, and other businesses when Asael Smith's family moved to the community.[23] Lucy met Joseph while working in a store that her brother owned in the town. Lucy and Joseph married on January 24, 1796.

President Brigham Young declared of this union,

> [It] was decreed in the counsels of eternity, long before the foundations of the earth were laid that [Joseph Smith] should be the man, in

21 Bushman, "Joseph Smith Family," 13.

22 Lucy Mack Smith, History, 1844–1845, bk. 2, [2], JSP.

23 LaMar E. Garrard, "Traditions of Honesty and Integrity in the Smith Family," in *Regional Studies in Latter-Day Saint Church History: The New England States*, ed. Donald Q. Cannon, Arnold K. Garr, Bruce A. Van Orden, and Brigham Young University (Provo, UT: Brigham Young University Religious Studies Center; Salt Lake City: Deseret Book, 2004), 108.

> the last dispensation of this world, to bring forth the word of God to the people and receive the fulness of the keys and power of the Priesthood of the Son of God. The Lord had his eye upon him, and upon his father, and upon his father's father, and upon their progenitors clear back to Abraham, and from Abraham to the flood, from the flood to Enoch, and from Enoch to Adam. He has watched that family and that blood as it has circulated from its fountain to the birth of that man.[24]

Mini-Devotional—Heavenly Father's Plan

Ponder the plan that Heavenly Father has in store for you and how he has prepared not only you but generations of your ancestors to fulfill his plan for you. Trust that everything your Heavenly Father has promised will be accomplished in his own way and timing.

- What blessings have you experienced by relying on Heavenly Father's timing?
- What blessings are promised to us as we strive to keep the commandments?

Thank Heavenly Father for the love he has for you and for knowing you well enough to discern when it is time for the major events of your life to be accomplished.

24 Ostler, "Glimpses of Church History," 185–86.

Joseph Smith Birthplace and Memorial Grounds and Monument, Sharon, Vermont

Joseph Smith Birthplace and Memorial Grounds in Sharon, Vermont. Photo by Casey Paul Griffiths.

After marrying, Joseph Smith Sr. and Lucy Mack Smith farmed in Tunbridge for the next six years before selling the property in 1802. While in Tunbridge, they had their first four children. Their first was an unnamed son who did not live past infancy. They then had Alvin in 1798, Hyrum in 1800, and their first daughter, Sophronia, in 1803. The family of five moved to Royalton for a few months and then to a farm in Sharon, Vermont, that they rented from Lucy's father, Solomon Mack.[25] While running this farm, Joseph also taught school during the winter months to make ends meet.

On December 23, 1805, Joseph Smith Jr., the Prophet of the Restoration, was born while his family still lived in Sharon. He was named Joseph, not only after his father but in fulfillment of prophecy given by Joseph of Egypt many centuries prior: "But a seer will I raise up out of the fruit of thy loins; and unto him will I give power to bring forth my word unto the seed of thy loins. . . . And his name shall be called after me; and it shall be after the name of his father. And he shall be like unto me; for the thing which the Lord shall bring forth by his hand, by the power of the Lord shall bring

25 Garrard, "Traditions of Honesty and Integrity," 111.

my people unto salvation" (2 Nephi 3:11, 15). This prophecy shows that Joseph Smith was foreordained for his role as a prophet in the latter days. He would translate the Book of Mormon from gold plates and restore the gospel of Jesus Christ in its fullness once more.

Joseph Smith Birthplace and Memorial Grounds in Sharon, Vermont. Photo by Casey Paul Griffiths.

The Smith family lived on the Sharon farm for three years, from 1804 to 1807. Solomon Mack later returned to the farm until the death of his wife, Lydia Gates Mack, around 1817. After her death, he returned to live in Gilsum with his son, Solomon Mack II.[26] The Sharon farm site is still a spot of significance to Latter-day Saints. The farm is now located on a 283-arce plot of land known as the Joseph Smith Memorial Grounds. Junius F. Wells, son of Daniel H. Wells, a close friend of Joseph Smith Jr. in Nauvoo, went to Vermont in 1884 to locate the site of the Prophet's birth. When he arrived, all he found was the hearthstone and the remaining foundation where the small house once stood.

Later, in March 1905, Junius F. Wells returned to New England to discuss his plan for building a monument to Joseph Smith Jr. with a contractor named Riley C. Bowers. Riley believed the idea was workable, and with this endorsement, Junius shared his idea with the First Presidency in a letter

26 Ostler, "Glimpses of Church History," 188–89.

dated April 1, 1905. The First Presidency answered that Junius should first locate the Prophet's birthplace and then try to purchase the land. Only then would they consider the proposal for the monument.[27]

These stones at the Joseph Smith Memorial mark the foundation of the small cabin where Joseph Smith, Jr. was born. Photos by Casey Paul Griffiths.

It was simple to find the land where Joseph Smith Jr. was born. Several residents of Sharon helped to identify the Solomon Mack property on May 19, 1905. The land was owned by C. H. Robinson, and Junius F. Wells bargained with Robinson to purchase the property and a narrow section of land connecting the birthplace site with Dairy Hill Road. After purchasing the sixty-eight acres, Junius returned to Salt Lake City and prepared a report for the First Presidency, complete with a sketch of the monument he had envisioned. He suggested the monument be 38½ feet tall and

27 Kay Godfrey, "Historical Cliffhanger: How We Came to Mark Joseph Smith's Birthplace," *Meridian Magazine*, December 28, 2018, https://latterdaysaintmag.com/historical-cliffhanger-how-we-came-to-mark-joseph-smiths-birthplace/.

be made of gray Barre granite. A tribute to the Prophet would be on the inscription die and the capstone. The First Presidency approved the project and publicly announced the monument on July 1, 1905. On July 6, Junius was given full power of attorney to erect the monument that would be known as the Joseph Smith Birthplace Memorial. From then on, Junius devoted himself to building the monument. He located a quarry in Barre, Vermont, wherein they found a granite piece that could be used for the monument's die and capstone. They found two pieces suitable for the first and second bases soon after.

Many challenges stood in the way of completing this project. Locating a forty-foot shaft of Barre granite was very difficult. The shaft they eventually found weighed sixty tons, and a temporary railroad was constructed to transport the stone. The shaft was transported six miles by train to the Barclay Brothers cutting and polishing shed. Once it arrived, it took only sixteen minutes to cut.

After the stone was polished, Junius F. Wells used a railroad line that ran from Barre to Royalton to transport the stone shaft. Then, to transport the shaft from Royalton to the monument site, Junius found a special wagon built to bring the stones to the site. The wagon had tires that were twenty inches wide, axles that were eight feet long and eight inches in diameter, and a total weight of eight tons. The bridge over the First Branch of the White River in South Royalton had to be reinforced to support the weight.[28] Twenty-two horses in total were sent to transport the first full load, which contained the monument's two base pieces. The progress was slow-moving as the horses would get tired and the wagon would sink into the mud. The crew transporting the load ended up wedging ten-by-three-inch hardwood planks under the wheels to keep them from getting stuck in the mud. The journey from Royalton to the monument site was only two miles, but it took two weeks before the bases made it to South Royalton and another week before they arrived at the monument site in late October 1905.

The next stone was the nineteen-ton, six-foot inscription die. They transported it without incident until they reached the bridge over the Tunbridge Branch. The wagon carrying the die was higher than what the covered bridge allowed. Fortunately, the contractor provided a special

28 Article on the history of the Joseph Smith Birthplace Monument, *Meridian Magazine*, December 28, 2018, Church History Library.

low-to-the-ground wagon which allowed the die to pass under the covered bridge. The die arrived successfully thanks to this small miracle.

The hearthstone from the original cabin where Joseph Smith, Jr. was born can be found in the visitor's center. Photo by Casey Paul Griffiths.

On November 7, 1905, the monumental task of hauling the forty-foot, forty-ton shaft began. The journey to the memorial site would take approximately thirty-three days, with the crew traveling only the length of a football field each day. Eventually they made it to the foot of Haynes Hill. It rained all that day, and the land was nothing but a muddy bog. It would be impossible to go further without a miracle. Junius knelt and prayed for a miracle before retiring to a hotel for the night. Junius's prayer was answered that evening. A very cold northeastern wind blew south out of Quebec, forming a Canadian Clipper that swept through Vermont, dropping the temperature to thirty-five degrees. The bog froze as hard as steel, which allowed the crew to transport the shaft up the hill. They managed to do it so quickly that the crew transporting the shaft arrived at the site a day before the inscription die did.[29]

The last stone to arrive at the site was the ten-ton molded cap. By November 26, 1905, all the stones were at the site. A derrick would lift the forty-foot shaft thirteen feet into the air, turn it perpendicular, and set it into place on the site. This was scheduled to be completed on December 8, 1905. On the day of the event, the assembled crowd cheered as the shaft was lowered into place. After giving a prayer of thanks, Junius F. Wells leaped to his feet and exclaimed, "All right boys, now I am with you, let her go!" After 137 days of grueling work and a series of miracles, the Joseph Smith Birthplace Monument was completed.[30]

The dedicatory services for the site were held on December 23, 1905, the hundredth anniversary of the Prophet's birth. Twenty-five Church leaders,

29 Godfrey, "Historical Cliffhanger."
30 Godfrey, "Historical Cliffhanger."

including the prophet, President Joseph F. Smith, traveled from Utah to participate. In his dedicatory prayer, President Smith referred to the granite shaft as an apt "token that inspired man to God whom [he] didst make into a polished shaft in [his] hand." Junius F. Wells returned to Vermont to the memorial the two summers following the dedication to supervise beautification of the monument. Though many Vermont residents opposed the monument at first, Junius observed a "lessening of prejudice" as visitors felt the "reverent spirit in the beautiful place."[31]

In 1913, the memorial's caretaker invited the missionaries and Latter-day Saints in New England to celebrate Pioneer Day in Sharon. Eastern States Mission President Ben E. Rich spoke of Joseph Smith Jr., who foretold of the Saints becoming a mighty people in the Rocky Mountains. He expressed how appropriate it was to celebrate the holiday at the Prophet's birthplace in light of this prophecy.[32]

Photo from the top of Patriarch Hill, the Joseph Smith Memorial Monument is visible in the distance.. Photo by Casey Paul Griffiths.

31 Richard O. Cowan, "Yankee Saints: The Church in New England During the Twentieth Century," in *Regional Studies in Latter-Day Saint Church History: The New England States*, ed. Donald Q. Cannon, Arnold K. Garr, Bruce A. Van Orden, and Brigham Young University (Provo, UT: Brigham Young University Religious Studies Center; Salt Lake City: Deseret Book, 2004), 176–77.

32 Cowan, "Yankee Saints," 176–77.

On the grounds now stands a memorial shaft raised to the Prophet. Visitors can also see the sites of the Mack family's original cabins. The original stone doorstep and a stone garden mark the approximate location where the birthplace home stood. There is also a chapel, a visitors' center, and camping facilities on site.[33] Elder B. H. Roberts, who served as president of the Eastern States Mission from 1922 to 1927, frequently took his missionaries to visit the site. On one occasion, he knelt with them at the crest of a nearby hill and reviewed instances in the past dispensations when the Lord had manifested himself on mountain tops. His mission secretary, Henry D. Taylor, recalled: "As he prayed his voice choked with emotion, tears filled his eyes, and a glow came into his face; his snow-white hair waved in the gentle breeze. As he continued pouring out his soul to the Lord, the veil grew very thin. Surely the Lord was near." After this experience, the hill that showed a compelling view of the green Vermont countryside in every direction was named Patriarch's Hill.[34]

Mini-Devotional—Enduring Trials

Ponder the trials that the Smith family experienced to come to the place where their son Joseph Smith Jr. would be born. Think about how these trials prepared them for the events and further trials that would follow as their son worked to restore the gospel of Jesus Christ.

- How have trials shaped your testimony in the Savior?
- How has God helped you in your trials?

Thank your Heavenly Father for your family and for the trials that they endured to be the people that you know in your life today. Ask Heavenly Father for the courage to overcome your own trials and to have faith that this will help you become the person you are meant to become.

33 Ostler, "Glimpses of Church History," 189.
34 Cowan, "Yankee Saints," 177.

Dartmouth College and the Site of Joseph Smith's Leg Surgery, West Lebanon, New Hampshire

View of the Mascoma River near where the leg operation was performed on Joseph Smith as a young boy. Photo by Casey Paul Griffiths.

This restaurant now stands on the site of the home where Joseph Smith's leg operations took place. Photo by Casey Paul Griffiths.

In 1811, when Joseph Smith Jr. was about five or six years old, the Smith family moved to a small, rented house in the town of Lebanon, New

Hampshire (now West Lebanon). The house they lived in for two years was located south of the Mascoma River and east of the Connecticut River, which separates the states of New Hampshire and Vermont. The year after moving, between 1812 and 1813, a plague of typhus fever swept through the area where the Smith family lived, and all of the Smith children fell ill with the disease. Joseph's sister Sophronia nearly died from the illness, and his brother Hyrum had to take leave from work for a full year to recover. Joseph himself suffered a variety of symptoms, which eventually morphed into an infection known as hematogenous osteomyelitis—an infection in the bone of his leg.[35]

Under normal circumstances in the 1800s, the cure for this infection would be to amputate the leg. However, Dr. Nathan Smith, founder of Dartmouth Medical School in Hanover, New Hampshire, developed a new medical procedure to treat the infection and still save the leg. Hyrum Smith was classmates with five of Dr. Smith's children, and it was likely through this connection that the Smith family was able to contact Dr. Smith and hire him with a team of surgeons and medical students to perform the operation that he had developed.[36] Before the operation, Dr. Smith wished to have Joseph bound to the bed and to have him take brandy or wine to help with the pain of the surgery. At that time, anesthesia had not been invented, but it was common for patients to drink some alcohol before being operated on. Joseph refused to be bound and refused to drink any alcohol, insisting instead that his father hold him on the bed and that his mother leave the room.

Lucy Mack Smith did not witness the surgery itself but kept account of the operation as it occurred.

> The surgeons began boring into the bone, first on one side of the affected part, then on the other after which, they broke it loose with a pair of forceps or pincers: thus they took away, 9 large pieces of the Bone. When they broke off the first piece, he screamed so loud with the pain <of his legs>, that I could not repress my desire <to> go<ing> to him but

35 "Smith Family History in West Lebanon, New Hampshire," *Ensign Peak Foundation Journal*, https://ensignpeakfoundation.org/west-lebanon-new-hampshire/.

36 "Joseph Smith's Leg Surgery in West Lebanon, New Hampshire," September 27, 2011, *Cannundrums Religion Blog*, cannundrum.blogspot.com/2011/09/joseph-smiths-leg-surgery-west-lebanon.html.

> as soon as I entered the room <he cried out> Oh! Mother! go back! go back! I do not want you to come in. I will tough it if you will go.[37]

After the surgery, Joseph recovered and regained his strength. Following an additional drainage of the bone, with fourteen pieces of bone working their way to the surface, the wound closed successfully. Not many other complications were mentioned on record.[38] Joseph spent the next three years on crutches and walked with a limp in his step for the rest of his life. The rented home where the surgery took place is no longer there, torn down in 1967, but the Mascoma River that ran close to the house can be viewed in various areas.

Mini-Devotional—Love of Families

Ponder the courage and strength Joseph Smith Jr. had to undergo the operation as well as the work of God's hand in this event. During this surgery and for the rest of his life, Joseph's family members were some of his strongest supporters. They mourned with him when he mourned, comforted him when he needed comforting, and were willing to stand as witnesses of God beside him.

- In what ways can you support family members who are struggling?

Pray and thank Heavenly Father for the advances in medicine that provide proper treatment and for the doctors that work to provide that treatment every day. Also pray for the Holy Ghost to help you find opportunities to serve your family.

---

37 Lucy Mack Smith, History, 1844–1845, bk. 3, [2], JSP.

38 LeRoy S. Wirthlin, "Joseph Smith's Boyhood Operation: An 1813 Surgical Success," *BYU Studies* 21, no. 2 (1981): 152.

Solomon Mack Home, Sharon, Vermont

Site of the Solomon Mack Home when Joseph Smith was born in 1805. Photo by Kenneth Mays.

Remnants of the foundation of the Solomon Mack home. Photo by Casey Paul Griffiths.

This sign marks the place of the old stone bridge near the Solomon Mack home. Photo by Casey Paul Griffiths.

The old stone bridge near the Solomon Mack home. Photo by Casey Paul Griffiths.

Foundational remnants of the Daniel G. Mack home. Photo by Casey Paul Griffiths.

Also remaining on the Joseph Smith Birthplace and Memorial Grounds is the cellar foundation of the home that was built by Lucy Mack Smith's father, Solomon Mack, around the year of 1805. The hundred-acre portion of land that he purchased bridged the towns of Royalton and Sharon, Vermont. In 1799, Solomon and his wife followed their two married children to Tunbridge to be closer to them. Between the years 1806 and 1811, while bedridden, Solomon studied the Bible closely and prayerfully. In his autobiography, he wrote of his own conversion to Jesus Christ and how the Lord's hand played a role through his trials and eventually brought him peace.[39]

Mini-Devotional—Small and Subtle Promptings of the Holy Ghost

Much like the trials and experiences that Joseph Smith Sr. and Lucy Mack Smith went through, Solomon Mack's own trials and experiences played a role in the early life of Joseph Smith Jr. While Joseph Smith Sr. and Lucy were continually moving around the state of Vermont to find stable work, Solomon was prepared to rent out an extra home on his property for the young family to live before they could find work elsewhere. As you look over the foundation site, surrounded by the wooden fence, think of how actions that seem less significant could have a bigger impact in a later day. Think about a time that a small action had a larger impact, whether for

39 Ostler, "Glimpses of Church History," 192.

yourself or for someone else. Even the smallest of actions can be part of a bigger picture that you cannot see right now.

- When was a time that a small act of kindness helped you or someone you loved?
- What are some things you can do to better recognize the promptings of the Holy Ghost?

Pray that the next time you feel the Holy Ghost prompting you, you will answer that prompting immediately. Pray for opportunities to serve others in your community and encourage others to do the same.

Brigham Young's Birthplace Monument, Whitingham, Vermont

Monument at Brigham Young's birthplace.. Photo by Kenneth Mays.

In addition to the Smith family a number of significant early families associated with the Restoration trace their ancestry this area. Brigham Young, the ninth of eleven children, began his life in a town in Whitingham, Vermont, about a hundred miles southwest of Sharon. The Young family also relocated many times to find work. Historians have not been able to pinpoint the exact location within Whitingham where Brigham was born, but they have narrowed it down to two pieces of land.

Originally, the Young family settled in Hopkinton, Massachusetts, where Brigham Young's father, John Young, was enlisted in the Continental Army to fight in the Revolutionary War. As their family grew, John and his wife, Nabby Howe Young, moved from Hopkinton to Platauva District of East Central New York (the area now known as Durham, Greene County) and again to Coxsackie, Albany County, New York, before returning to Hopkinton in 1790. Between 1786 and 1799, eight children were born to the Young family.

They moved again, this time to Whitingham, Vermont, in 1801. John Young's older sister, Susannah Young, married Joseph Mosley Sr., who ran a business of dividing, selling, and buying acres of land in Whitingham. John Young purchased a spot of land in Whitingham from his brother-in-law and moved his family, except for one of his daughters, Rhonda (she stayed in Hopkinton with her paternal grandparents for unknown reasons), onto the land within two months.[40] Nabby Howe Young would give birth to their ninth child, Brigham, not long after settling. They did not stay on the land for long and moved to back New York when Brigham was just two years old.

While the exact location of the John Young cabin in Whittingham is unknown today, a stone memorial has been placed at the approximate site of Brigham Young's birthplace. No one knows who placed the memorial there, but it was placed sometime before the year 1900. It reads: "Brigham Young, born on this spot 1801, a man of much courage and superb equipment."[41] On May 28, 1950, President George Albert Smith dedicated a larger twelve-foot-high marker to honor that area of Vermont as President Young's birthplace. On that day, President Smith prayed,

> We are here to do honor to one of thy faithful sons who in the past so lived that there are hundreds of thousands of people who honor him and revere his memory. We are here now to present this monument of granite,

---

40 Larry C. Porter, "Brigham Young's Birthplace in Whitingham, Vermont," in *Regional Studies in Latter-Day Saint Church History: The New England States*, ed. By Donald Q. Cannon, Arnold K. Garr, Bruce A. Van Orden, and Brigham Young University (Provo, UT: Brigham Young University Religious Studies Center; Salt Lake City: Deseret Book, 2004), 121–24.

41 Ostler, "Glimpses of Church History," 198.

> the native granite of this great state, that which President Brigham Young himself undoubtedly would choose if he were here, and Heavenly Father, we pray that thy Spirit may remain here that those who come to read the inscription on the monument may realize that thou are the Father of us all and that he whom we are gathered to honor was one of thy sons who was great enough to assume his responsibilities and carry a tremendous load during his long lifetime.[42]

Mini-Devotional—Staying True to the Faith

In 1832, Brigham Young was baptized in the newly restored Church of Jesus Christ. From the time of his baptism to his apostleship, and later ordination as the second President of The Church of Jesus Christ of Latter-day Saints, Brigham remained one of the most loyal and faithful early members of the Church. He courageously defended Joseph Smith Jr.'s role as the Prophet of the Restoration and defended the divinity and authenticity of the Book of Mormon against not only the Church's enemies but even against fellow Apostles who apostatized from the Church.

- How can you better recognize when you are being tempted?
- In what ways can you defend your testimony when it is challenged?

Though today we may not face angry mobs driving us from our homes, there are many distractions and temptations surrounding us that can be just as dangerous. As you walk along the grassy hills that surround the monument of Brigham Young's birthplace, ponder your own spiritual journey on earth and what has led you to develop your own testimony of Jesus Christ, the Book of Mormon, and the Restoration. Think of ways that you can courageously defend your faith, even in the face of great adversity.

Pray for inspiration to identify distractions that could cause you to waver in your testimony, and ask for strength to stand against those who will work to weaken and destroy it. Also pray for courage to be valiant in your testimony at all times, in all things, and in all places.

42 George Albert Smith, "Dedicatory Prayers at the Unveiling Ceremonies," *Improvement Era*, September 1950, 693.

Home of Ezra and Sarah Carter, Scarborough, Maine

The Fox Islands. Photo by Kenneth Mays.

Wilford Woodruff is considered one of the greatest missionaries of all time to serve in the Church and to spread the gospel of Jesus Christ. One of his best-known missions was in the 1840s when he traveled to England and converted nearly a thousand people to the restored gospel. He also served a mission in 1837 to the Fox Islands in Maine. Though not as well known as his missions to England, Wilford's Fox Islands mission is still important in Church history. His zeal, initiative, and ability to follow the promptings of the Holy Ghost ensured his success.

The Fox Islands consist of two islands along the coast of Maine, midway between the New Hampshire state line and the Canadian border. They are about twelve miles out in the open water of the Penobscot Bay. Today the islands are known as North Haven (North Fox Island) and Vinalhaven (South Fox Island). Wilford Woodruff likely became familiar with these islands thanks to his wife, Phebe Carter Woodruff, and her family, who were residents of Scarborough, Maine. Wilford met Phebe in January 1837 and married her that April, only two and half months later, in the home of Joseph Smith Jr. He was called to serve as a missionary a few weeks later. As he prepared to depart, Wilford felt greatly inspired to select the Fox Islands as his area of labor. He said, "I made my feelings known to the Apostles, and they advised me to go."[43]

While on the way to the Fox Islands, Wilford Woodruff and his companion, Jonathan Hale, performed missionary work anywhere they could. They labored in Canada, New York, Connecticut, Massachusetts, and New Hampshire. They made special effort to contact friends and family they knew in those areas. The people they visited included Wilford's brothers, Azmon and Thompson Woodruff in Richland, New York; his sister, Eunice, in Colebrook, Connecticut; Titus Woodruff in Avon, Connecticut; and even Wilford's parents in Farmington, Connecticut. Some of these family members Wilford had not seen in several years.

When the companionship made it to Maine, Phebe Carter Woodruff joined the elders in teaching her mother and father, Ezra and Sarah Carter, who lived in Scarborough. Wilford Woodruff met and taught the Carters on August 8, 1837. Although the Carters did not accept the gospel or the invitation to be baptized when their son-in-law taught them, they were sympathetic to the messengers that brought them the gospel. They remained cheerful administrators to "the elders of Israel and the Saints of God, in their travels in the world."[44]

Mini-Devotional—Acts of Service

Though not owned by the Church, Ezra and Sarah Carter's home in Scarborough still stands today. As Wilford Woodruff and Jonathan Hale stayed in this home on their way to the Fox Islands, Phebe Carter Woodruff joined them, hoping to share the restored gospel with her closest family. While the Carters did not accept the restored gospel during their mortal lives, they remained faithful to their own faith in Jesus Christ and served those that approached them, whether they were traveling elders from the Church or other Latter-day Saints that crossed their path.

- What are ways you can serve others in your community?

---

43 Donald Q. Cannon, "Wilford Woodruff's Mission to the Fox Islands," in *Regional Studies in Latter-Day Saint Church History: The New England States*, ed. by Donald Q. Cannon, Arnold K. Garr, Bruce A. Van Orden, and Brigham Young University (Provo, UT: Brigham Young University Religious Studies Center; Salt Lake City: Deseret Book, 2004), 148–50, 167.

44 Ostler, "Glimpses of Church History," 199.

- What are ways you can be a disciple of Christ in your day-to-day activities?
- How is serving your neighbor equivalent to serving God?

There are many people who share this same commitment to serving their fellow men, whether they accept the restored gospel or not. Ponder ways in which you can contribute to the less fortunate in your own community or even in your own neighborhood. Recall the scripture Mosiah 2:17: "And behold, I tell you these things that ye may learn wisdom; that ye may learn that when ye are in the service of your fellow beings ye are only in the service of your God."

Pray for opportunities to serve your neighbors and truly minister to those around you. Ask your bishop or Church leaders about those who are struggling and make plans to serve those members and help them feel God's love.

Baptist Church, North Haven, Maine

Baptist Church where Wilford Woodruff preached in New Haven, Maine. Photo by Kenneth Mays.

Wilford Woodruff and Jonathan Hale arrived at the northern end of the Fox Islands, North Haven, on the morning of August 20, 1837. After finding food and lodging, the missionaries made their way to a Baptist chapel and meetinghouse, the only one located on the island. They made arrangements with the minister of that church to preach to his congregation at five o'clock that evening. Curiosity about the arrival of the two strangers led most of the church's congregation to attend the special session. The two missionaries spoke with great power and conviction as they testified that God had once again raised up a prophet and established his Church on the earth. They continued to preach about the Restoration of the gospel for four more evenings. The minister that granted them access to the meetinghouse, Mr. Newton, accepted the message and listened a witness of its truthfulness. However, despite this, Newton chose to reject the truth and fight against the missionaries instead. He recruited the Methodist minister in Vinalhaven, Mr. Douglas, to join him in his campaign. However, even with the opposition of the two ministers, Wilford and Jonathan were successful in baptizing more than a hundred residents of the Fox Islands.[45]

Wilford Woodruff continued to preach to many people on the mainland of Maine, traveling with his wife to Bangor, Searsmont, Camden, and Belfast. He returned to the Fox Islands in 1838, and while there, he received a letter from the President of the Quorum of the Twelve, Thomas B. Marsh, informing Wilford that he had been appointed as a member of the Quorum of the Twelve Apostles and that he was instructed to finish his mission and return to Missouri on April 26 the following year. When he returned to Missouri, Wilford brought along with him fifty-three Latter-day Saints he had helped baptize.

Mini-Devotional—Joy in the Work

Like many other missionaries in the early Church and now, Wilford Woodruff faced persecution and hardship as he worked to spread the restored gospel of Christ throughout the world. However, despite this opposition, there are many miracles that await those that continue to do the work.

- How can you find joy in the work when facing opposition?
- What are ways you can love others who have different beliefs than you?

As you observe this Baptist chapel where Wilford Woodruff preached, think of the strength these men had as they endured slander, lies, and other

45 Ostler, "Glimpses of Church History," 199–200.

obstacles and still continued to preach their message. Think of the diligence they developed as they listened to what others said about them and how they countered these claims through strong testimony and faith in their Savior and the restored gospel.

Thank Heavenly Father for the strong leaders of our Church, both local and general. Each has been selected by God to be a witness of Jesus Christ and to teach us the Lord's will. Thank Heavenly Father for your own trials that have helped to shape you into the person you are today, and pray for the strength to overcome more as your life continues.

Significant events at this location:

- Appearance of the Angel Moroni on September 21, 1823.
- Joseph Smith first brought the gold plates to his family's home on September 21, 1827.
- Joseph's first efforts at translation took place at this location.
- The eight witnesses saw and handled the gold plates at the Smith farm.
- Doctrine and Covenants 2, 19, 22, 23, and 32 were all received at or near the Smith farm.

THE JOSEPH SMITH FAMILY FARM

The rebuilt Joseph Smith Sr. Family Log Home. The current structure stands in the footings of the original log home where the Angel Moroni appeared to Joseph Smith. Photo by Casey Paul Griffiths.

Between 1816 and 1817, Joseph Smith, Sr. and Lucy Mack Smith, moved their family to a small farm on the outskirts of Palmyra, New York. They immediately began saving to make the first payment on a 100-acre lot of forested land on the border of Palmyra and Manchester township. During these early years in Palmyra, the Smith family labored to clear the thick forest off their property and create a small wheat farm. The Smith's remained on their Palmyra farm until 1830, when they were directed by revelation to gather to Kirtland, Ohio (see Doctrine and Covenants 30).

At the time the Smith's moved to the Palmyra area, western New York was known as the "burned over district" because of an intense series of religious revivals that took place in the area. The recent completion of the Erie Canal brought scores of new settlers to the region. Like the Smiths, many of these settlers were religious seekers, searching for meaning and higher connection to God. The term "burnt-over district" was first used by Charles Grandison Finney, who remarked, "I found that region of country what, in the western phrase, would be called a 'burnt district.' There had been, a few years previously, a wild excitement passing through that region, which they called a revival of religion."[46] In his own history, Joseph Smith, Jr. recalled "an unusual excitement on the subject of religion" in the area, later commenting, "the whole district of country seemed affected by it, and great multitudes united themselves to the different religious parties, which created no small stir and division amongst the people, some crying, 'Lo, here!' and others, 'Lo, there!'" (Joseph Smith-History 1:5).

During the time the Smiths lived on their Palmyra farm, a number of key events took place that began the process of the restoration of the Church of Jesus Christ. In 1820, in a grove somewhere on the property Joseph Smith saw a vision of God the Father and Jesus Christ. In 1823, Joseph was visited by the Angel Moroni, who showed him the location of the sacred record of the Nephites. Joseph retrieved the plates in 1827 and began the process of translation while living on the Smith farm, but was soon forced to flee because of intense persecution. After the translation was completed, Joseph returned to the Smith farm, and it was here that he showed the plates to the Eight witnesses of the Book of Mormon.

46 Charles Grandison Finney, *Autobiography of Charles G. Finney,* 1908, Kindle edition, p. 67.

The Smith Family Log Home[47]

Upstairs rooms in the Smith Family Log Home. Photo by Casey Paul Griffiths.

In the winter of 1818 to 1819, Joseph Sr. and Lucy moved the ten members of their family into a small log cabin, approximately 1,000 square feet in size. The Smiths lived here from 1818 to 1825, when they built a larger frame house just down the road.[48] The Smiths were living in this cabin when Joseph had his First Vision in the spring of 1820 (Joseph Smith-History 1:14). But perhaps the most significant event associated with the log cabin is the visitation of the Angel Moroni on September 21, 1823.

In Joseph's earliest history, written in 1832, he describes the appearance of the personage by writing, "When I was seventeen years of age I called again upon the Lord and he shewed unto me a heavenly vision for behold an angel of the Lord came and stood before me and it was by night and he called me by name and he said that the Lord had forgiven me my sins."[49]

47 For an in-depth study of the history, archaeological research, and reconstruction of the Smith Family Log Home, see T. Michael Smith, "Reconstructing the Smith Family Log Home," in *Artifacts Speak,* ed. Glen M. Leonard, (Provo, UT: BYU Studies, 2021), 29-61.

48 See Donald L. Enders, "A Snug Log House," *Ensign,* August 1985.

49 History, circa summer 1832, 4, JSP.

While Joseph wrote several detailed descriptions of Moroni's visit, the most detailed account comes from his close associate Oliver Cowdery. In 1835 Oliver wrote a series of letters written to W. W. Phelps, who published then in the *Latter-day Saints' Messenger and Advocate.* These letters provide further insight into Joseph's mindset before the visitation of Moroni. Oliver writes, "Our brother's mind was unusually wrought up on the subject which had for so long agitated his mind—his heart was drawn out in fervent prayer, and his whole soul was so lost to every thing of a temporal nature, that earth, to him had lost it claims and all he desired was to be prepared in heart to commune with some kind of messenger who could communicate to him the desired information of his acceptance with God." Oliver adds, "The stature of this personage was a little above the common size of men in this age; his garment was perfectly white, and had the appearance of being without seam."[50]

Joseph described the angel as follows: "He had on a loose robe of most exquisite whiteness. It was a whiteness beyond anything earthly I had ever seen; nor do I believe that any earthly thing could be made to appear so exceedingly white and brilliant. His hands were naked, and his arms also, a little above the wrist; so, also, were his feet naked, as were his legs, a little above the ankles. His head and neck were also bare. I could discover that he had no other clothing on but this robe, as it was open, so that I could see into his bosom. Not only was his robe exceedingly white, but his whole person was glorious beyond description, and his countenance truly like lightning. The room was exceedingly light, but not so very bright as immediately around his person. When I first looked upon him, I was afraid; but the fear soon left me" (Joseph Smith-History 1:32-32).

Joseph's lengthy description of the angel's appearance contributes to our understanding of the nature of resurrected beings. As the most prominent of the angelic messengers sent to carry out the work of the Restoration in the latter days, Moroni is an attestation to the hopeful doctrine of not just a resurrected Savior but a resurrection for all of the sons and daughters of God. The physicality of Moroni and the other angels of the Resurrection demonstrates the ongoing miracle of the resurrection of Jesus Christ. Not only does Jesus Christ live, but thousands—perhaps millions—have been given a renewed life in a physical body because of the Savior and His

50 "Letter IV," February 1835, 78–80.

Atonement. A later revelation to Joseph will teach that the righteous of former days "were with Christ in his resurrection" (D&C 133:54). Moroni is the vanguard of an army of physical, resurrected beings who will assist in the work of preparing the earth for the millennial reign of Christ, when all will be resurrected.

Moroni's prophesied that Joseph's name "should be had for good and evil among all nations, kindreds, and tongues" is remarkable for its accuracy and fulfillment. A person may doubt the prophetic claims of Joseph Smith, but there is no denying that Moroni's prophecy has come to pass. A simple internet search shows the vast number of people who speak evil of the Prophet's words and deeds as well as the millions who sustain him as a Prophet of God and the instrument used by Jesus Christ to restore the true Church to the earth.

View of the Smith Family Log Home, where the Angel Moroni appeared to Joseph Smith. Photo by Kenneth Mays.

Harold Bloom, a noted literary critic and professor of humanities at Yale University, wrote extensively on Joseph Smith's life and teachings. Though he never joined the Church, Bloom wrote, "I also do not find it possible to doubt that Joseph Smith was an authentic prophet. Where in all of American history can we find his match? The Prophet Joseph has proved again that economic and social forces do not determine destiny. … In proportion to his importance and his complexity, he remains the least-studied personage, of an undiminished vitality, in our entire national saga."[51]

As Joseph states in his history, what he has written is only a sample of the visitation, which "occupied the whole of that night" (Joseph Smith—History 1:47). In his 1835 account of Moroni's visitation to Joseph Smith, Oliver Cowdery quoted from a number of other biblical passages, including Deuteronomy 32:23–24, 43; Psalms 100:1–2; 107:1–7; 144:11–12; 144:13; 146:10; Isaiah 1:23–26; 2:1–4; 4:5–6; 11:15–16; 29:11, 13–14; 43:16; Jeremiah 16:16; 30:18–21; 31:1, 8–9, 27–28, 32–33; 50:4–5; and 1 Corinthians 1:27–29. Because of his close association with Joseph Smith, it is likely that Oliver knew more about the visitation of Moroni than anyone except the Prophet. However, in the account that Oliver wrote in the *Messenger and Advocate* it is difficult to tell when he is quoting the angel and when he is explaining the themes emphasized by Moroni in this visitation.[52]

Interior of the Smith Log Home. Photo by Kenneth Mays.

Most of the passages emphasized in both Joseph's and Oliver's accounts of Moroni's visit reference the gathering of Israel in the last days. For instance, the passage quoted most liberally in Oliver's account is Jeremiah 31, in which the Lord promises the following: Behold, the days come, said the

51 Harold Bloom, *The American Religion,* (New York: Simon & Schuster, 1992), 95.

52 See Kent P. Jackson, "Moroni's Message to Joseph Smith," *Ensign*, August 1990.

Lord, that I will make a new covenant with the house of Israel, and with the house of Judah: Not according to the covenants that I made with their fathers in the day that I took them by the hand to bring them out of the land of Egypt; which my covenant they brake, although I was an husband unto them, saith the Lord: But this shall be the covenant that I will make with the house of Israel; After those days, saith the Lord, I will put my law in the inward parts, and write it in the their hearts; and will be their God, and they shall be my people (Jeremiah 31:31–33).

While the log home was the site of many important events in early Church history, it was also the location of the most severe tragedy that struck the Smith family during their time in Palmyra. On November 19, 1823, the eldest son in the Smith family, Alvin, became ill and died in the log home. For more information on this, see chapter on the Martin Harris farm and Alvin Smith grave.

The Smith family left their snug log cabin around 1825, when their frame home, located just down the road was completed. For a time, Hyrum Smith and his new bride Jerusha made their home in the log cabin. The log home went out of their ownership when the Smiths left Palmyra in 1830. The location of the log cabin was rediscovered during an archaeological excavation of the area in 1982. The current log home on the Smith farm is a recreation built in 1997-1998. The structure was dedicated by President Gordon B. Hinckley on March 27, 1998. During the dedication President Hinckley highlighted the importance of the log home when he said, "this will do away with the legend that has somewhat grown up among us that the other house [the Smith frame home] was the place where Moroni visited the Prophet. It was in this place and in the upstairs room that that even occurred."[53]

Mini-Devotional – God's Work for You

Joseph later said that when Moroni appeared to him it was three years after the First Vision. Joseph said he prayed "that [he] might know of my state and standing before him" (Joseph Smith-History 1:29).

53 Greg Hill, "President Hinckley dedicates historic sites," *LDS Church News,* March 4, 1998.

- Why is it important to pray continually to know our state and standing before God?
- What does this teach us about Joseph's humility that he wanted to know his standing before God?

When Moroni appeared to Joseph Smith when he was just seventeen years old and told him "that God had a work for me to do; and that my name should be had for good and evil among all nations, kindreds, and tongues, or that it should be both good and evil spoken of among all people" (Joseph Smith-History 1:33).

- What do you think is the work God has given you to do?
- How has Moroni's prophesy that Joseph's name should "both good and evil spoke of among all people" been fulfilled?

Joseph Smith Sr. Frame Home[54]

The Joseph Smith Sr. Frame home is the original structure the Smiths lived in when Joseph received the plates. It has been restored to its 1820s appearance. Photo by Casey Paul Griffiths.

54 For a detailed history of the Smith Family Frame Home, see Donald L. Enders, Rediscovering the House That Alvin Built: The Joseph Smith Sr. Family Frame Home at Manchester, New York," (Provo, UT: BYU Studies, 2021), 61-111.

Located just down the road from the Smith family's log cabin is their frame home, completed around 1825. The frame home is the original structure and has been restored to its appearance around the time that the Smiths lived in the home. After living in their cozy log home for several years, the Smiths commenced construction on a larger frame home in November 1822. The Smiths moved into this home in 1825 and were living here during some of the key events linked to the coming forth of the Book of Mormon.

Alvin Smith took the lead in building the new family home. Lucy Mack Smith later recalled, "Alvin [Smith] was very much animated by the idea as he said of making father and mother so comfortable, he would say, 'I am going to have a nice pleasant room for them to sit in and everything arranged for their comfort, and they shall not work as they have done any more."[55] Tragically, construction on the home was dealt a serious setback when Alvin passed away in 1823. The Smiths hired Russell Stoddard, a local carpenter, to assist them in completing the home. The family continued working on the house, even moving into it before the home was fully enclosed.[56] Lucy Mack Smith reported summarized the move by saying, "ere long we had a pleasant commodious habitation ready to receive us."[57]

The Smiths were living in this home in September 1827 when Joseph Smith retrieved the plates from the nearby Hill Cumorah. After receiving the plates from the Angel Moroni on 21 September, Joseph hid them in the woods between the Smith home and the hill. During this time there was intense interest in the plates in the Palmyra area, and several local men made attempts to steal the plates. Lucy Mack Smith later explained, "It now seemed that Satan had stirred up the hearts of those who had in any way got a hint of the Matter to search into it and make every possible move towards preventing the work."[58] Lucy even explained that Willard Chase, a local neighbor, had hired a "conjuror" from over sixty miles away to divine "by magic art" the place where the plates were hidden.[59]

During this time Lucy Mack Smith was overwhelmed with anxiety over the safety of the plates. When Joseph saw her distress, he spoke to her privately, telling her he had a "key" to know that the record was safe. She

55 "Lucy Mack Smith, History, 1844–1845, Page [3], bk. 4," p. [3], bk. 4, JSP.

56 Enders, 74-76.

57 "Lucy Mack Smith, History, 1844–1845, Page [9], bk. 4," p. [9], bk. 4, JSP.

58 Lucy Mack Smith, History, 1844–1845, Page [8], bk. 5," p. [8], bk. 5, JSP.

59 "Lucy Mack Smith, History, 1844–1845, Page [8], bk. 5," p. [9], bk. 5, JSP.

later recalled, "I knew not what he meant but took the article in my hands and examining it - with no covering but a silk handkerchief - found that it consisted of two smooth three cornered diamonds set in glass and [inside] silver bows."[60] This is the only recorded instance of Joseph showing the Nephite interpreters to a family, and likely took place inside the Smith home.

Facsimile of the Nephite interpreters and the gold plates. Photo by Casey Paul Griffiths.

Eventually Joseph decided to retrieve the plates from their hiding place in the woods and bring them to the Smith home. The plates weighed around fifty pounds, making it challenging for Joseph carry them. Aware of the people seeking to steal the plates, Joseph ducked off the main road and chose instead to travel through the woods. On his way he was accosted by a man "who demanded the plates, and struck him with a club on his side"[61] Joseph pivoted and knocked the man to the ground, running away as quickly as he could while carrying the record. After running for about another half mile, Joseph was attacked by another man, but managed to escape. He was attacked a third time before he arrived at the house, striking

60 "Lucy Mack Smith, History, 1844–1845, Page [7], bk. 5," p. [7], bk. 5, JSP.

61 Joel Tiffany, "Mormonism," *Tiffany's Monthly,* August 1859, 165, quoted in Michael Hubbard MacKay and Gerrit J. Dirkmaat, *From Darkness Into Light,* (Salt Lake: Deseret Book, 20150, 12.

his attacker so forcefully that he dislocated his thumb."[62] Katherine Smith, Joseph's sister, later remembered that when Joseph arrived at the house he was "nearly exhausted, carrying the package of the gold plates . . . clasped to his side with his left hand and arm, and his right hand was badly bruised." Joseph handed the plates through the window to Josiah Stowell, his former employer and a close friend. Stowell later said he was the "first person that took the plates out of [Joseph Smith's] hands the morning [he] brought them in."[63]

During the next few weeks the plates were kept hidden in the Smith home. During this time Joseph used the Nephite Interpreters to protect the plates. Lucy Mack Smith later said that Joseph "could at any time ascertain the approach of danger either to himself or the record and for this cause he kept these things constantly about his person."[64] One day when Joseph was working on the farm with his father, he was alerted through the interpreters that a group of hostile men were approaching the home. Before the men arrived, Joseph and his family removed the hearthstone near the fireplace and dug a hole underneath large enough to hold the plates and the wooden box they were being stored in. As soon as they had secured the plates, a large group of men approached the house, Joseph and his finished burying the plates. They quickly devised a plan to startle their adversaries, with Joseph and his younger brother running to the door screaming at the top of their lungs. This startled the men, who fled in disarray.[65]

---

62 "Lucy Mack Smith, History, 1844–1845, Page [11], bk. 5," p. [11], bk. 5, JSP.

63 Mackay and Dirkmaat, 13.

64 "Lucy Mack Smith, History, 1844–1845, Page [1], bk. 6," p. [1], bk. 6, JSP.

65 Mackay and Dirkmaat, 15.

Interior of the Smith Frame home. Photo by Kenneth Mays.

During the time the plates remained in the Smith home, several of Joseph's family members had the opportunity to touch, lift, or hold the plates or the box they were stored in. Katherine Smith later said she was cleaning the house when she saw 'a package on the table containing the gold plates." She picked them up to judge the weight, later saying they were "heavy like gold." She even said that she "rippled her fingers up the edge of the plates and felt that they were separate metal plates and heard the tinkle of the sound they made."[66] William Smith, who was a teenager at the time, later said that he "hefted the plates as they lay on the table wrapped in an old frock or jacket in which Joseph had brought them home."[67] From their recollections, it appears that Katherine and William never saw the plates directed, but handled them and examined them under a covering. During the time the plates were in the Smith home, most of Joseph's closest family and friends said they were able to physically lift or heft the plates.[68]

While the plates were in their home, the Smiths were constantly interrupted by visitors who attempted to locate or steal the plates. Samuel

66 "The Prophet's Sister Testifies She Lifted the B of M Plates," *Messenger,* (Berkley, CA), October 1954, quoted in MacKay and Dirkmaat, 15.

67 *Early Mormon Documents,* ed. Dan Vogel, 1:505 and 508.

68 MacKay and Dirkmaat, 15.

Lawrence, another Palmyra local, came to the Smith home demanded to take the plates. When Joseph refused to negotiate, Lawrence later returned with another local man in possession of a divining rod. Lawrence and the rodsman walked into the west room of the home, and the rodsman point his rod towards the family fireplace, stating that the plates were under the hearthstone. Lawrence and the rodsman left the home without the plates, but Joseph soon removed them from their hiding place under the hearthstone, placing them in his father's coopershop near the barn. Joseph hid the box the plates were kept in as a decoy under the floor panels of his father's shop. He then hid the plates themselves in a large pile of flax in the loft of the shop. On a morning soon after Joseph found the floorboards torn up and the decoy box smashed.

Keeping the plates on their farm was at times a terrifying experience for the Smith family. Katherine Smith later told her granddaughter about an evening when a group of men rushed into the Smith home intent on stealing the plates. Joseph, seeing the men coming, wrapped the plates in a linen frock and thrust them into Katherine's arms, telling her "Take these quickly and hide them." Katherine and her sister Sophronia ran to bedroom near the kitchen, got into bed, and pulled back the covers. Placing the plates between them, the girls pretended to be asleep while the men searched the house. One even went into the bedroom where they were sleeping, shining a lantern and looking under the bed for the plates. When the men failed to find them they left, leaving the two girls undisturbed.[69]

Eventually persecution in Palmyra became so intense, the Joseph chose to take the plates to Harmony, Pennsylvania, where his in-laws lived. The majority of the translation of the Book of Mormon took place in Harmony and in Fayette, New York. The Smith family remained in Palmyra and was visited several times during the translation of the Book of Mormon. In fact one of the key events linked to the coming forth of the Book of Mormon took place on the Smith farm.

69 Donald L. Enders, Rediscovering the House That Alvin Built: The Joseph Smith Sr. Family Frame Home at Manchester, New York," (Provo, UT: BYU Studies, 2021), 105-16. This incident is not referred to by Lucy Mack Smith or Joseph Smith, is a second-hand account recorded by Katherine Smith's granddaughter, Mary Salisbury Hancock. There is no reason to disbelieve it, but because it comes from only one source it should be used cautiously.

Mini-Devotional – The Importance of Family

Throughout his life, Joseph's family were some of his strongest supporters. They shared in his triumphs and failures, and helped him protect the gold plates from the people trying to steal them. Joseph's father and mother allowed the plates to be kept safe in their home. Joseph's sisters and brothers also helped him keep the plates safe. Even on his deathbed Alvin gave Joseph encouragement telling him "I want you to be a good boy and do everything that lays in your power to obtain the records be faithful in receiving instruction and keeping every commandment that is given you."[70]

- How has your family been a support to you?
- How can your family help you overcome the challenges you face?

Oliver Cowdery and the Smith Farm

Even while Joseph was working on the translation in Pennsylvania, the Smiths continued to play a key role in bringing about the Restoration. In the Fall of 1828, a young man named Oliver Cowdery came to stay with the Smith family. Oliver spent a year boarding with the Smith family in Palmyra, where he served as a local schoolteacher. While staying with the Smiths he was introduced to the work Joseph was engaged in. The Prophet's 1838 history states, "After we had received this revelation [D&C 6] he [Oliver Cowdery] stated to me that after he had gone to my father's to board, and after the family communicated to him concerning my having got the plates, that one night after he had retired to bed, he called upon the Lord to know if these things were so, and that the Lord had manifested to him that they were true."[71] In his 1832 history, Joseph wrote that the "Lord appeared unto a young man by the name of Oliver Cowdery and shewed unto him the plates in a vision and also the truth of the work and what the Lord was about to do through me his unworthy servant."[72] This appearance likely took place in the Smith home.

70 "Lucy Mack Smith, History, 1844–1845, Page [4], bk. 4," p. [4], bk. 4, JSP.
71 JS History, vol. A-1, 13, JSP
72 History, circa Summer 1832, 6, JSP

Joseph Smith Sr. also played a key role in helping Oliver find his role in the work. Lucy Mack Smith recorded, "One day, Oliver came home from school in quite a lively mood; as soon as he had an opportunity of conversing with Mr. Smith [Joseph Smith Sr.] he told him that he [Oliver] had been in deep study all day and it had been put into his heart that he would have the privilege of writing for Joseph when the term of school which he was then teaching was closed."[73] It appears the Lord manifested himself to Oliver in a number of ways to enlist his services in the work.[74]

Mini-Devotional – Receiving Revelation

When the Lord spoke to Oliver Cowdery in section 6 of the Doctrine and Covenants, He told him "if you desire a further witness, cast your mind upon the night that you cried unto me in your heart, that you might know concerning the truth of these things. Did I not speak peace to your mind concerning the matter? What greater witness can you have than from God?" (D&C 6:22-23). Oliver may have been surprised to find that he had already received a revelation from God, he just hadn't realized that he had received one!

- What can you do to better recognize when God speaks to you?
- What is a time when you have received revelation from God?

Oliver may have been surprised because he was expected something more dramatic than just peace to his mind. It is important to recognize that when God speaks to us, He uses gentle means to communicate that can be missed if we aren't carefully paying listening.

73 Lucy Mack Smith History, 1844–1845, bk 8, 1, JSP.

74 Some material from this section was previously published as Casey Paul Griffiths, *Doctrine and Covenants Minute,* Doctrine and Covenants 6, doctrineandcovenantscentral.org, accessed January 11, 2022.

The Eight Witnesses and the Smith Farm

Facsimile of the gold plates. Photo by Kenneth Mays.

Another important event that took place on the Smith farm is the experience of the Eight Witnesses of the Book of Mormon. We do not know precisely where on the Smith farm that this even took place, but Lucy Mack Smith, identified the farm as the place where Joseph Smith showed the plates to the Eight Witnesses. John Whitmer later said the experience took place "in Joseph Smith's house" which makes it likely that the event took place in the Smith Log Cabin.[75] This event occurred shortly after the experience where the three witnesses saw the Angel Moroni, beheld the plates and other sacred relics (see D&C 17), and heard the voice of God testifying of the truthfulness of the Book of Mormon.

Lucy Mack Smith recorded, "The following day we returned, a cheerful, happy company; and in a few days we were followed by Joseph, Oliver, and

75 "Death of John Whitmer," *Deseret News,* August 14, 1878, in Larry E. Morris, *A Documentary History of the Book of Mormon,* (New York: Oxford University, 2019), 452-455. Because of Alvin's death, their rising debt, and the dishonest dealings of a land agent, the Smith's were forced from their frame home and were residing in the Log Home when the Book of Mormon was published in 1830. See "Sacred Grove and the Smith Family Farm," Church History Topics, churchofjesuschrist.org, accessed January 14, 2022.

the Whitmers, who came to make us a visit, and make some arrangements about getting the Book printed. Soon after they came, all of the male part of the company, together with my husband, Samuel [Smith], and Hyrum [Smith], retired to a place where the family were in the habit of offering up their secret devotions to God. They went to this place because it had been revealed to Joseph that the plates would be carried thither by one of the ancient Nephites: Here it was that those eight witnesses, whose names are recorded in the Book of Mormon, looked upon them and handled them."[76]

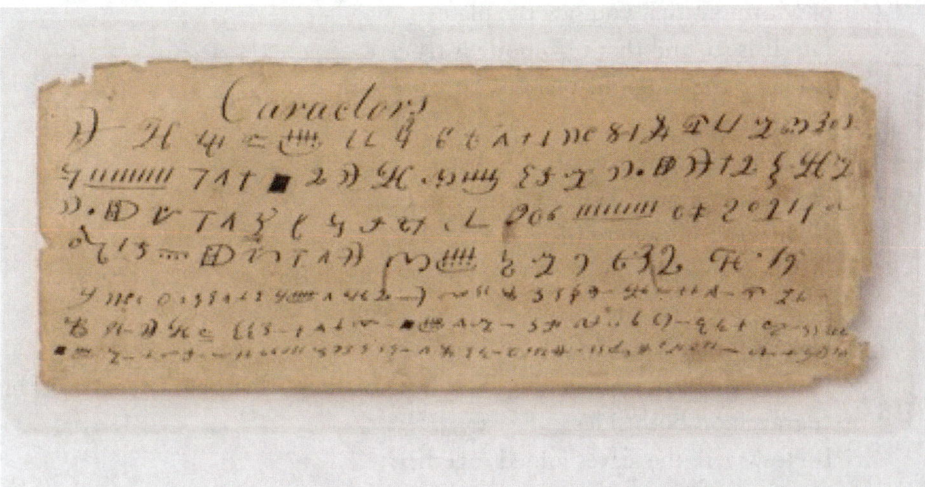

The "Caracters" document was consists of characters copied from the gold plates, probably by John Whitmer, one of the Eight Witnesses of the Book of Mormon. Photo by Cordale Ottley, courtesy Community of Christ.

The Eight Witnesses of the Book of Mormon are Christian Whitmer, Jacob Whitmer, Peter Whitmer, Jr., John Whitmer, Hiram Page, Joseph Smith Sr., Hyrum Smith, and Samuel H. Smith. All of the Eight Witnesses were members of the Smith or Whitmer families (Hiram Page was a brother-in-law, married to Katherine Whitmer). In contrast to the Three Witnesses, who had a supernatural experience, the Eight Witnesses had a physical experience with the plates. Their testimony, included in every copy of the Book of Mormon, included their statement the witnesses not only saw the plates but "did handle with our hands" adding "we also saw the appearance of ancient work, and or curious workmanship."[77]

76 "Lucy Mack Smith, History, 1845," p. 155-156, JSP.
77 "Testimony of Eight Witnesses," *Book of Mormon.*

In an interview conducted near the end of his life, John Whitmer gave the most detailed description of the experience the Eight Witnesses had with the plates. P. Wilhelm Poulson, a reporter from the *Deseret News* in Utah, visited John Whitmer's home in Far West, Missouri. Poulson later wrote, "John Whitmer received me as a dear father would receive a son, and answered readily all my questions." Poulson then recorded their interview as follows:

> I said: I am aware that your name is affixed to the testimony in the Book of Mormon, that you saw the plates?
> He–It is so, and that testimony is true.
> I–Did you handle the plates with your hands?
> He–I did so!
> I–Then they were a material substance?
> He–Yes, as material as anything can be.
> I–They were heavy to lift?
> He–Yes, and you know gold is a heavy metal, they were very heavy.
> I–How big were the leaves?
> He–So far as I recollect, 8 by 6 or 7 inches.
> I–Were the leaves thick? He–Yes, just so thick, that characters could be engraven on both sides.
> I–How were the leaves joined together?
> He–In three rings, each one in the shape of a D with the straight line towards the centre. I-In what place did you see the plates.
> He-In Joseph Smith's house; he had them there.
> I–Did you see them covered with a cloth?
> He–No. He handed them uncovered into our hands, and we turned the leaves sufficient to satisfy us.
> I-Were you all eight witnesses present at the same time?
> He-No. At that time Joseph showed the plates to us, we were four persons, present in the room, and at another time he showed them to four persons more....
> when Joseph Smith [III]...sent word to John Whitmer to reaffirm his testimony, his answer was: 'I have never recalled it, and I have nothing to reaffirm.'

The Eight Witnesses suffered serious persecution because of their experience with the plates. David Whitmer recalled seeing Hiram Page being beaten by a mob because of his testimony. Whitmer said, "While the mob was raging in Jackson Co., [Missouri] in 1833 some young men ran down Hiram Page in the woods, one of the eight witnesses, and commenced beating and pounding him with whips and clubs. He begged, but there was no mercy. They said he was a damned Mormon, and they meant to beat him to death! But finally one [of] them said to him, if you will deny that damned book, we will let you go. Said he, how can I deny what I know to be true? Then they pounded him again. When they thought he was about to breathe his last they said to him, 'Now what do you think of your God, when we don't save you[?]'"[78]

None of the Eight Witnesses every denied their testimony of seeing the plates, though their lives took them in varying directions in the coming years. Christian Whitmer was the first of the Eight Witnesses to pass from this life, dying in 1835. Only a year later, Peter Whitmer, Jr., died only a year later. Both were serving faithfully in the Church at the time of their death. After their deaths Oliver Cowdery wrote of both of them: "They were the first to embrace the new covenant, on hearing it, and during a constant scene of persecution and perplexity, to their last moments, maintained its truth – they were both included in the list of the eight witnesses of the Book of Mormon, and though they have departed, it is with great satisfaction that we reflect that they proclaimed to their last moments, the certainty of the former testimony."[79]

---

78 William E. McLellin, "W.E. McLellan's Book, January 4, 1871," in Morris, 444.

79 "The Closing Year," *Latter-day Saints' Messenger and advocate,* December 1836, 426, in Morris, 446-447.

The Eight Witnesses Monument in Liberty, Missouri. Two of the Eight Witnesses, Christian Whitmer and Peter Whitmer, Jr. are buried near the monument. Photo by Casey Paul Griffiths.

Jacob Whitmer, John Whitmer and Hiram Page all became disaffected from the Church in 1838. None of them ever returned, but none ever denied their testimony of the Book of Mormon. Even after they left the Church and became embittered towards Joseph Smith and other Church leaders, they never wavered. When Hiram Page was asked in 1847 about his experience with the plates he wrote, "As to the Book of Mormon, it would be doing injustice to myself, and to the work of God of the last days, to say that I could know a thing to be true in 1830, and know the same thing to be false in 1847."[80]

80 Hiram Page, quoted in Larry E. Morris, *A Documentary History of the Book of Mormon,* (New York: Oxford University, 2019), 425-426.

This first edition copy of the Book of Mormon belonged to Samuel H. Smith, one of the Eight Witnesses of the Book of Mormon. Photo by Cordale Ottley, courtesy Reid Moon.

Joseph Smith, Sr., Hyrum Smith, and Samuel H. Smith, the Prophet's father and brothers, never denied their testimony and died firm in the faith. Hyrum Smith once said that he would rather die "than deny the things which my eyes had seen, which my hands had handled, and which I had borne testimony to, wherever my lot had been cast."[81] Joseph Smith, Sr., died in Nauvoo surrounded by his family and friends in 1840. Hyrum Smith died as martyr in Carthage Jail in 1844. The day he died he was studying the Book of Mormon (see D&C 135:4-5). Samuel H. Smith died just a month after Joseph and Hyrum in July 1844. He remained proud of his testimony throughout his life. A copy of the Book of Mormon owned by Samuel Smith and today in the hands of a private collector show that

81 Letter, Hyrum Smith "to the Saints scattered abroad," December 1839, *Times and Seasons* 1, no. 2 (Decewmber 1839), 20, 23, in Morris, 426.

someone, likely Samuel himself, drew a large star next to his name in the list of witnesses.

Though their lives went in different directions, the Eight Witnesses remained bonded through the profound experience they shared on the Smith farm with the Prophet and the sacred record. In 1836 John Whitmer wrote, "I have most assuredly seen the plates from whence the Book of Mormon is translated, and that I have handled these plates, and know of a surety that Joseph Smith, jr., has translated the Book of Mormon by the gift and power of God."[82]

Mini-Devotional – Standing As Witnesses of God

Detail of the Eight Witnesses on the Angel Moroni monument on the Hill Cumorah. Photo by Casey Paul Griffiths.

The Eight Witnesses never denied their testimony of the Book of Mormon, though they faced terrible persecution. Today their witness is carried in every copy of the Book of Mormon and has been shared throughout all the world. Think about your own witness of the gospel, particularly the Book of Mormon.

- What experiences have helped you strengthen your testimony of the Gospel?

82 John Whitmer, "ADDRESS To the patrons of the Latter Day Saints' Messenger and Advocate," *Latter Day Saints' Messenger and Advocate* 2, No. 6 (March 1836): 286-287, in, Morris, 425-426.

- How can you serve as a witness of the things you know to be true?

The Smiths Leave Their Farm

The expense of building the frame home, the death of Alvin Smitha, and the duplicitous dealings of a dishonest land agent forced the Smith family to lose the title to their farm. When the time the Book of Mormon was published in 1830, the Smiths had moved back to the log cabin and were reduced to serving as tenant farmers on the land they had labored so hard to clear. The left the area for good in 1831 when they obeyed the Lord's command to "assemble together at the Ohio" (D&C 37:3).[83]

The Smith Family Farm came back into Church hands in the early 20th century. In 1905, Church President Joseph F. Smith visited the farm. Moved by the spirit of the site, he began making arrangements to purchase it, and two years later the farm was obtained by the Church. A young couple, Willard and Rebecca Bean, were called on a mission to manage the property.[84] Their mission marked the return of the Church to the Palmyra region. During the ensuing decades the number of visitors increased until restoration began on the farm beginning in the 1980s. After leaving the farm Lucy Mack Smith reflected wistfully on their time in Palmyra and "the busy bustling life we had lad and the apparent prospect of a quiet and comfortable old age."[85] Instead of the quiet life they intended, the Smiths left their peaceful farm as they were swept up the grand drama of the Restoration.

83 "Sacred Grove and the Smith Family Farm," Church History Topics, churchofjesuschrist.org, accessed January 14, 2022.

84 "Sacred Grove and the Smith Family Farm," Church History Topics, churchofjesuschrist.org, accessed January 14, 2022.

85 "Lucy Mack Smith, History, 1844–1845, Page [11], bk. 4," p. [11], bk. 4, JSP.

Significant events at this location:

- The Smiths farmed roughly sixty acres of their hundred-acre property and kept about forty acres for a wood lot. Historians believe that the Sacred Grove was within the original forty-acre wood plot, and the grove currently spans ten to twelve acres.
- Joseph Smith Jr. saw God the Father and his son Jesus Christ at this site early in the spring of 1820.
- Joseph showed the gold plates to the Eight Witnesses near the Sacred Grove.
- There are still trees in the Sacred Grove that date back to the time of the First Vision; these are referred to as "witness trees."

THE SACRED GROVE

The Sacred Grove on the Smith Family Farm. Photo by Casey Paul Griffiths.

Joseph Smith struggled to record the events of his life because of his limited schooling. He explained, "I was deprived of the benefit of an education suffice it to say I was merely instructed in reading writing and the ground rules of Arithmetic which const[it]uted my whole literary acquirements."[86] Therefore, it is not surprising that he did not immediately record what happened to him on that early spring morning in 1820. Joseph wrote of the insufficient nature of language in a letter to William W. Phelps, asking God to "deliver [them] in [his] due time from the little narrow prison

86 Joseph Smith History, ca. Summer 1832, p. 1, JSP.

almost as it were total darkness of paper pen and ink and a crooked broken scattered and imperfect language."[87]

Joseph Smith recorded details of his First Vision experience in eight different documents, three of which are duplicates of a previous one with only minor differences. Reading the Prophet's own words in these accounts most often increases the reader's testimony. As historian Dean C. Jessee commented:

> In the process of reading through the documents and writings of Joseph Smith over the years, my conviction of the credibility of his story and the nature of his mission has increased immensely. The evidence has built detail upon detail, document upon document, to the point where it has become a compelling reality to me. Once I was able to separate the thoughts Joseph Smith put on paper with his own hand from those written by others for him, there was a whole new light cast upon him. I found that his personal writings—few in number compared to his entire archive—were like a vein of gold threading through a mountain. I saw in them a different spirit; I saw a sensitive, caring man whose prose was born of religious experience. I could well believe his words when he said: "I had actually seen a light, and in the midst of that light I saw two Personages, and they did in reality speak to me."[88]

Joseph was the only human witness of the First Vision, and his direct accounts are therefore invaluable. If we want to know more about Joseph and his feelings and emotions, if we want to know more about the nature of this young man, reading his own words will enhance our understanding.

87 Joseph Smith Jr. to William W. Phelps, November 27, 1832, p. 4, JSP.

88 Dean C. Jessee, "The Earliest Documented Accounts of Joseph Smith's First Vision," in *Exploring the First Vision*, ed. Samuel Alonzo Dodge and Steven C. Harper (Provo, UT: Brigham Young University Religious Studies Center, 2012), 4.

Religious Fervor in Palmyra, New York

Brook between the Smith log home and the Sacred Grove. Photo by Casey Paul Griffiths.

In setting the scene for the First Vision, Joseph Smith recounted that in Palmyra, New York, where he lived, there was "an unusual excitement on the subject of religion . . . which created no small stir and division amongst the people." Converts and priests alike manifested great zeal, causing a "scene of great confusion and bad feeling ensued" with "a contest about opinions" (Joseph Smith—History 1:5–6). This "time of great excitement" caused Joseph to feel great uneasiness and confusion about "who was right and who was wrong" (Joseph Smith—History 1:8). Then one day he read in his Bible: *"If any of you lack* wisdom, *let him ask of God, that giveth to all men liberally, and upbraideth not; and it shall be given him" (James 1:5). The scripture had a great influence on him. He recounted:*

> Never did any passage of scripture come with more power to the heart of man than this did at this time to mine. It seemed to enter with great force into every feeling of my heart. I reflected on it again and again, knowing that if any person needed wisdom from God, I did; for how to act I did not know, and unless I could get more wisdom than I then had, I would never know; for the teachers of religion of the different

> sects understood the same passages of scripture so differently as to destroy all confidence in settling the question by an appeal to the Bible.
>
> At length I came to the conclusion that I must either remain in darkness and confusion, or else I must do as James directs, that is, ask of God. I at length came to the determination to "ask of God," concluding that if he gave wisdom to them that lacked wisdom, and would give liberally, and not upbraid, I might venture. (Joseph Smith—History 1:12–13)

Mini-Devotional—Searching for Truth

As you visit the Sacred Grove and read Joseph Smith—History, found in the Pearl of Great Price, you may feel that Joseph Smith was not only a prophet of God but also a literary genius. The twenty-six verses written about the First Vision are excellent prose and could be considered the single greatest piece of history ever written. Those verses also teach us much about determining the difference between fact and opinion and about searching for truth. Joseph used two words that begin with the letter *p* to help us know when people might be trying to convince others to adopt their opinions. When we recognize these techniques, we should raise a red flag of caution and be aware of deceit.

One technique of persuasion focuses on the intellect. Joseph Smith described the priests of his day using this practice: "The Presbyterians were most decided against the Baptists and Methodists and used all the powers of both reason and sophistry to *prove* their errors, or, at least, to make the people think they were in error" (Joseph Smith—History 1:9; emphasis added). Sometimes when people teach opinions to seekers of truth, the teachers will try to prove their case. Such a sterile scholarly approach is manipulating, leading converts to heated debates rather than to peace and truth.

Others will use the technique of promoting their cause by evoking strong emotional responses. Joseph Smith described the Palmyra priests showing "great love and zeal," and they were "active in getting up and *promoting* this extraordinary scene of religious feeling, in order to have everybody converted" (Joseph Smith—History 1:6; emphasis added). Joseph noted that these "seemingly good feelings of both the priests and the converts were more pretended than real," and such expressions of love were used as a manipulation tactic and did not come from a sincere desire for conversion. People who want to share opinions as truth will often promote their cause. If someone is simply trying to tug at your heart strings, you should be concerned about their intentions; the truth needs no promotion. People who attempt to share their opinion as truth very often will either promote strong emotional responses or try to prove their point with sophistry and reason.

- Have you ever felt that someone was trying to prove that their opinion was truth?
- Have you ever felt that someone was promoting their opinion by trying to play on your emotions?

We can discern between truth and opinion by using Joseph Smith—History as an example. Those who speak the truth will not have to prove or promote their cause; instead, they will simply present the facts. In his writing, Joseph Smith was controlled in presenting the facts. He simply said, "For I had seen a vision; I knew it, and I knew that God knew it, and I could not deny it" (Joseph Smith—History 1:25). People who teach truth always present it without promotion or proof.

- What other verses in Joseph Smith—History show the young Prophet presenting the truth?
- How can you present your testimony rather than promote or prove it?[89]

89 S. Michael Wilcox, "What We Learn from Joseph Smith—History about Revelation" (Education Week lecture, Brigham Young University, 1999).

The Religious Struggles of Joseph Smith Sr. and Lucy Mack Smith

The four corner churches in downtown Palmyra. Each church consists of a different denomination. Photo by Richard Crookston.

Before Joseph Smith could restore the gospel, he had to turn his heart to his parents, and the very act of doing so brought about the First Vision. It was family turmoil that brought Joseph to his knees.

Lucy Mack Smith was very religious; she dreamed dreams and recorded them. As a teenager, one of her sisters was extremely ill and was cured miraculously by prayer. In 1803, Lucy became extremely ill, so much so that Joseph Smith Sr. thought his wife was going to die. Lucy pleaded with the Lord to spare her so she could raise her children. She recorded her experience: "My mind was much agitated during the whole night. Sometimes I contemplated heaven and heavenly things, then my thoughts would turn upon those of earth—my babes and my companion. During the night I made a solemn covenant with God that if he would let me live, I would endeavor to serve him according to the best of my abilities. Shortly after this I heard a voice say to me, 'Seek and ye shall find, knock and it shall be opened unto you. Let your heart be comforted, ye believe in God, believe also in me.'"[90] After she recovered from her illness, Lucy tried to find a church to attend. She was desperate for religion. However, during her search, her

90 Lucy Mack Smith, History, 1845, p. 40, JSP.

husband did not believe that any of the ministers of the churches she was visiting were following the precepts of the gospel found in the Bible.

Joseph Smith Sr.'s religious views were dramatically different from his wife's. He had seven of what he called visions, and from these he felt that the churches of his day were empty and hollow. In his dreams he would find himself in a desolate world or a gloomy desert. The desolation would open up to a garden where he would see a tree representing the love of God which rose at the end of a path leading away from the gloom. From these experiences, Joseph had a yearning to find God and salvation, but he felt it was not in the churches of his day.

Lucy Mack Smith, going against her husband's wishes, joined the Western Presbyterian Church in Palmyra. Her children Hyrum, Sophronia, and Samuel all attended with her, leaving Joseph Jr. and the other children at home with Joseph Smith Sr.

Joseph Smith Jr. was disturbed about this divisive situation. He was left to question who was right—his mother or his father? One might imagine that Joseph, after the First Vision, ran into the house and shouted the news to his mother that her church was false. Instead, his words to his mother were simply, "I have learned for myself that Presbyterianism is not true."

Have you ever wondered why Mother and Father Smith both accepted Joseph Smith Jr.'s story so faithfully? The trials that followed the First Vision might have divided any other family, but instead they united the Smiths. The First Vision brought answers that both of Joseph's parents were seeking, and as he turned his heart to his parents, the gospel was restored.

The First Vision did not occur simply because Joseph Smith read James 1:5. Rather, it happened after months of spiritual struggle. Beginning at age twelve, Joseph wanted to settle the differences between his mother and father's religious beliefs:

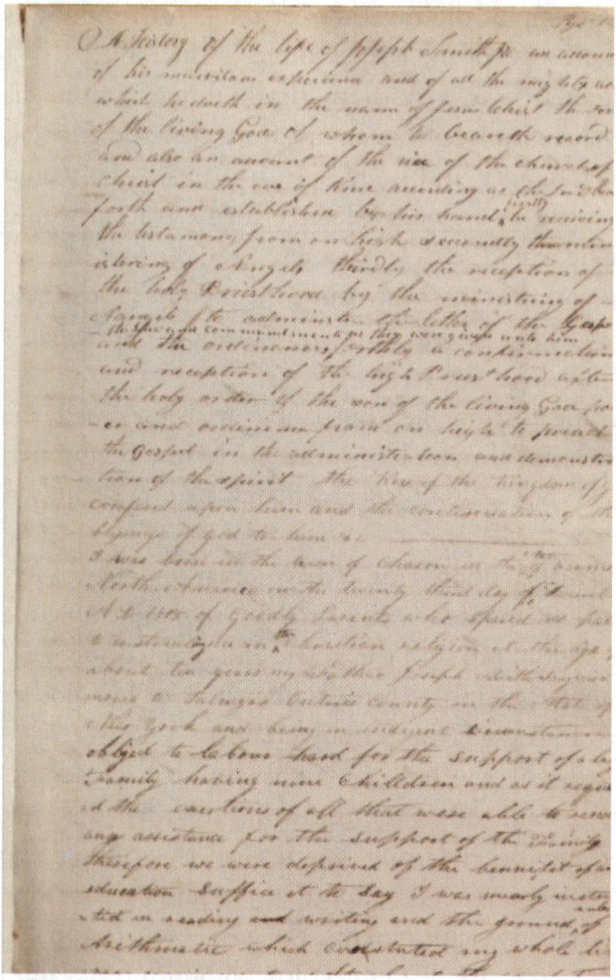

The earliest account of the First Vision, written by Joseph Smith in 1832. Photo courtesy of Joseph Smith Papers.

From the age of twelve years to fifteen I pondered many things in my heart concerning the situation of the world of mankind contentions and divi[si]ons wicke[d] ness and the abominations and the darkness which pervaded the of the minds of mankind my mind became exceedingly distressed for I become convicted of my sins and by searching the scriptures I found that man <mankind> did not come unto the Lord but they had apostatized from the true and living faith and there was no society or denomination that built upon the gospel of Jesus Christ as recorded in the New Testament and I felt to mourn for my own sins and for the sins of the world I learned in the scriptures that God was the same yesterday today and forever that he was no respecter of persons.[91]

Joseph finally decided to make his family division a matter of prayer. When he went to that familiar spot in the woods near his home, he wanted to know three things as he bowed in prayer: "(1) He was concerned for his own salvation and sought forgiveness of his sins; (2) he was concerned for the welfare of mankind in general, for, he said, 'I felt to mourn for my own

91 Joseph Smith History, ca. Summer 1832, in Letterbook 1, p. 2, JSP.

sins and for the sins of the world'; and (3) he wanted to know which, if any, of the churches was right, and which he should join."[92]

Mini-Devotional—Seeking the Lord's Direction

We hear much about being self-sufficient and self-confident, but when is it appropriate to seek the Lord's assistance? Through his account of the First Vision, Joseph Smith Jr. described those conditions in which we need the Lord's help:

- Have you felt great uneasiness about something?
- Have you felt great desire about an issue?
- Are you in a great confusion about something in your life?
- Do you need to reach a certain conclusion, and you do not know what the conclusion should be?
- Do you not know what is right or what is wrong with a certain situation?
- Do you need more wisdom?
- Have you come to a point in your life when you do not know which direction you should take?
- Can you come to a certain conclusion without God's help? (see Joseph Smith—History 1:8–10)[93]

If you have those kinds of questions about a situation in your life, let Joseph's experience of seeking guidance from the Lord be an example to you: you are right to ask the Lord for help.

92 James B. Allen and John W. Welch, "The Appearance of the Father and the Son to Joseph Smith in 1820," in *Exploring the First Vision*, ed. Samuel Alonzo Dodge and Steven C. Harper (Provo, UT: Brigham Young University Religious Studies Center, 2012), 67–69.

93 S. Michael Wilcox, "What We Learn from Joseph Smith—History about Revelation."

The Distraction of the Devil

Shadows in the Sacred Grove. Photo by Casey Paul Griffiths.

Reflecting on his experiences leading up to the First Vision, Joseph Smith stated: "It was the first time in my life that I had made such an attempt, for amidst all my anxieties I had never as yet made the attempt to pray vocally" (Joseph Smith—History 1:14). While Joseph's prayer in the Sacred Grove might not have been the first time that he had ever prayed, he stated that it was the first time that he had prayed aloud.

After kneeling down in the Sacred Grove, Joseph Smith struggled to pray as the adversary filled his mind with negative distractions. Orson Hyde wrote of the experience: "The adversary then made several strenuous efforts to cool his ardent soul. He filled his mind with doubts and brought to mind all manner of inappropriate images to prevent him from obtaining the object of his endeavors."[94] In addition to the mental attack from the adversary, there was also a physical distraction. Joseph said, "I heard a noise behind me, like some person walking towards me. I strove again to pray but could not. The noise of walking seemed to draw nearer. I sprung up on my feet and looked around but saw no person or thing that was

94 Orson Hyde, *Ein Ruf aus der Wüste* (A Cry out of the Wilderness), 1842, English translation, The Joseph Smith Papers, accessed May 21, 2022, JSP.

calculated to produce the noise of walking."[95] Also, as he felt thick darkness gather around him, he felt he was doomed to sudden destruction (Joseph Smith—History 1:15).[96] Joseph then recounted, "Exerting all my powers to call upon God to deliver me out of the power of this enemy which had seized upon me, and at the very moment when I was ready to sink into despair and abandon myself to destruction—not to an imaginary ruin, but to the power of some actual being from the unseen world, who had such marvelous power as I had never before felt in any being—just at this moment of great alarm, I saw a pillar of light," which held the greatest vision in human history (Joseph Smith—History 1:16).

Mini-Devotional—How to Pray

In the First Vision account, Joseph Smith taught us how to pray. As you think about your prayer habits, you could ask yourself the following questions:

- Am I alone where I will not be interrupted?
- Have I thought of an appropriate place to pray?
- Am I praying vocally?
- Am I kneeling?
- Am I offering up the desires of my heart or just words and thoughts?
- Have I exerted all my power to call upon the Lord?
- How often have I brought this to the Lord's attention?
- Have I labored to get an answer?
- Do I have a specific object in mind?
- Have I given the matter serious reflection?
- How deep is my desire?
- Are my feelings poignant?
- Is my mind partial to a certain decision?
- Have I acted on any suggestion I have found in the scriptures?
- Do I intend to act on the answer?

---

95 Joseph Smith, Journal, 1835–1836, p. 23, JSP.

96 Orson Pratt, *A[n] Interesting Account of Several Remarkable Visions, and The Late Discovery of Ancient American Records* (Edinburgh: Ballantyne and Hughes, 1840), [3]–[5], JSP.

- Have I gone to the scriptures for an answer? (see Joseph Smith—History 1:10–18)[97]

The Pillar of Light

Light reflects off leaves in the Sacred Grove. Photo by Casey Paul Griffiths.

At that moment of greatest alarm, Joseph Smith recounted that he found himself gazing into heaven when he saw "a pillar of light exactly over [his] head, above the brightness of the sun, which descended gradually until it fell upon [him]. It no sooner appeared than [he] found [himself] delivered from the enemy which held [him] bound" (Joseph Smith—History 1:16). In other accounts, Joseph associated this pillar of light with fire. He observed that as the light drew nearer to him,

> It increased in brightness, and magnitude, so that, by the time that it reached the tops of the trees, the whole wilderness, for some distance around was illuminated in a most glorious and brilliant manner. He expected to have seen the leaves and boughs of the trees consumed, as soon as the light came in contact with them; but, perceiving that it did not

97 S. Michael Wilcox, "What We Learn from Joseph Smith—History about Revelation."

> produce that effect, he was encouraged with the hopes of being able to endure its presence. It continued descending, slowly, until it rested upon the earth, and he was enveloped in the midst of it.[98]

Consuming nothing, the fire rested upon the earth and upon Joseph, surrounding or enveloping him in light.[99]

The Appearance of the Father and the Son

Joseph Smith wrote, "When the light rested upon me I saw two Personages, whose brightness and glory defy all description, standing above me in the air. One of them spake unto me, calling me by name and said, pointing to the other—*This is My Beloved Son. Hear Him!" (Joseph Smith—History 1:16–17; italics original).*

In other accounts, Joseph Smith provided more detail about the appearance of the Father and the Son. Alexander Neibaur remembered Joseph telling him that he "saw a fire towards heaven came near & nearer saw a personage in the fire light complexion blue eyes a piece of white cloth drawn over his shoulders his right arm bear after a while a other person came to the side of the first."[100] One other clarification Joseph gave was that our Heavenly Father and his son Jesus Christ looked very much alike. He said that the two beings "exactly resembled each other in feature, and likeness, surrounded with a brilliant light which eclipsed the sun at noon-day."[101] In another record, Joseph called this experience his "first visitation of angels." He said that he "saw many angels in this vision" on the early spring day in 1820.[102] Joseph also remembered that the Son declared to him that his sins were forgiven during the vision.

It is important that we understand what Joseph Smith learned when he saw the Father and the Son. First, he received the "knowledge of the reality of Christ, as one of the two personages pointed to the other and said, 'This is my Beloved Son, Hear him.'. . . Second, he learned that the Father and the Son knew him personally, for one of them (seemingly the Son) called

98 Pratt, *A[n] Interesting Account*, p. [3], JSP.

99 "Church History," in *Times and Seasons*, March 1, 1842, JSP.

100 Alexander Neibaur, Journal, May 24, 1844, p. [23], JSP.

101 "Church History," in *Times and Seasons*, March 1, 1842, JSP.

102 Joseph Smith, Journal, 1835–1836, p. 23, JSP.

him intimately by name, 'Joseph <my son>,' and told him, 'Thy sins are forgiven thee.'"[103]

Which Church Is True?

As Joseph Smith came to his senses after seeing the most glorious beings, he remembered why he was praying: "My object in going to inquire of the Lord was to know which of all the sects was right, that I might know which to join. No sooner, therefore, did I get possession of myself, so as to be able to speak, than I asked the Personages who stood above me in the light, which of all the sects was right (for at this time it had never entered into my heart that all were wrong)—and which I should join" (Joseph Smith—History 1:18). Alexander Neibaur remembered that Joseph also asked the Personages, "Must I join the Methodist Church[?]" The reply was: "They are not my People, all have gone astray there is none that doeth good no not one, but this is my Beloved Son harken ye him."[104] Joseph recorded: "I was answered that I must join none of them, for they were all wrong; and the Personage who addressed me said that all their creeds were an abomination in his sight; that those professors were all corrupt; that: 'they draw near to me with their lips, but their hearts are far from me, they teach for doctrines the commandments of men, having a form of godliness, but they deny the power thereof.' He again forbade me to join with any of them; and many other things did he say unto me, which I cannot write at this time" (Joseph Smith—History 1:19–20). The message for Joseph was that "all the religious denominations were believing in incorrect doctrines, and that none of them was acknowledged of God as his church and kingdom. And [that he] was expressly commanded to 'go not after them,' at the same time receiving a promise that the fulness of the gospel should at some future time be made known unto [him]."[105]

Joseph Smith "learned something more about the current state of Christianity as the Lord confirmed Joseph's personal conclusion, reached through study of the scriptures, about the Great Apostasy, namely that all churches had gone astray. Even before going into the grove, he understood

103 Allen and Welch, "Appearance of the Father and the Son," 72.

104 Alexander Neibaur, Journal, May 24, 1844, p. 23, JSP (spelling in original).

105 Joseph Smith, "Latter Day Saints," in *He Pasa Ekklesia*, ed. Rupp, 405, JSP.

that the gospel had been preached originally in truth and purity, but that the world had strayed from it." He was told that an apostasy had created a religious culture of false doctrine, sin, and corruption. "He was further commanded, to wait patiently until some future time, when the true doctrine of Christ and the complete truth of the gospel would be revealed to him. The vision closed and peace and calm filled his mind."[106]

The Aftermath of the First Vision

Panoramic view of the Sacred Grove. Photo by Casey Paul Griffiths.

According to scripture, it is impossible for any person to behold deity with natural eyes (see John 1:18; Doctrine and Covenants 67:10–13; Moses 1:2). However, purified and filled with the Spirit of God, Joseph Smith was able to stand in the presence of God and behold his glory; but it left him without any strength (Joseph Smith—History 1:20). This profound experience had a physically exhausting effect upon him, and when he endeavored to stand up, he felt uncommonly feeble. On the other hand, the mental and spiritual effect of this first theophany on Joseph was that he felt "comforted, and his mind was left 'in a state of calmness and peace, indescribable.' Joseph said in his earliest account, 'My soul was filled with love and for many days I could rejoice with great Joy and the Lord was with me.'"[107]

Joseph Smith also recounted, "Soon recovering in some degree, I went home. And as I leaned up to the fireplace, mother inquired what the matter was. I replied, 'Never mind, all is well—I am well enough off.' I then said to my mother, 'I have learned for myself that Presbyterianism is not true'"

106 Orson Hyde, *Ein Ruf aus der Wüste* (A Cry out of the Wilderness), 1842, English translation, JSP.

107 Allen and Welch, "Appearance of the Father and the Son," 77.

(Joseph Smith—History 1:21). This statement was an "understandable, yet courageous thing for a young boy to emphasize to his mother, who had recently converted to Presbyterianism." Others he shared with immediately afterwards were not as affable.[108]

We do not know who he told about the First Vision, but Joseph Smith did record that he was met with "persecution, contention, competition, religious excitement, bad feelings, strife, contempt, bitterness, hatred, and rejection."[109] Joseph was surprised that he was being attacked from almost every avenue: "I soon found, however, that my telling the story had excited a great deal of prejudice against me among professors of religion, and was the cause of great persecution, which continued to increase; and though I was an obscure boy, only between fourteen and fifteen years of age, and my circumstances in life such as to make a boy of no consequence in the world, yet men of high standing would take notice sufficient to excite the public mind against me, and create a hot persecution; and this was common among all the sects—all united to persecute me" (Joseph Smith—History 1:22).

The clergy Joseph Smith shared with met his story with an immediate negative response. A few days following the vision, Joseph shared his experience with a Methodist preacher who "treated [his] communication not only lightly but with great contempt, saying it was all of the devil, that there was no such thing as visions or revelations in these days; that all such things had ceased with the apostles, and that there never would be any more of them" (Joseph Smith—History 1:21). The preacher's premises included the following:

- Joseph's story was of the devil.
- There were no such things as revelations in what Dickens called "the age of railways."
- Visions or revelations ceased with the Apostles.
- There would never be any more visions or revelations.[110]

As Moroni prophesied, Joseph Smith's "name should be had for good and evil among all nations, kindreds, and tongues, or that it should be both

108 Allen and Welch, "Appearance of the Father and the Son," 47.

109 Allen and Welch, "Appearance of the Father and the Son," 55.

110 Steven C. Harper, "Evaluating Three Arguments Against Joseph Smith's First Vision," in *Exploring the First Vision*, ed. Samuel Alonzo Dodge and Steven C. Harper (Provo, UT: Brigham Young University Religious Studies Center, 2012), 308–9.

good and evil spoken of among all people" (Joseph Smith—History 1:33). After Joseph walked out of the Sacred Grove, no one could stand on neutral ground when it came to the First Vision and Joseph Smith.

Mini-Devotional—Preparing for Intense Trials

Joseph Smith displayed great faith when he prayed in the Sacred Grove, and that faith was tested in many ways after his First Vision theophany. The same happens to many of us when we demonstrate a little faith. Intense trials seem to come to us especially after we have just received revelation and are trying to accomplish good. Elder Jeffrey R. Holland explained:

> [The adversary uses] strong, *preliminary, anticipatory* opposition to many of the good things that God has in store for us. . . . "It isn't over until it's over." . . .
>
> . . . Opposition . . . often comes *after* enlightened decisions have been made, *after* moments of revelation and conviction have given us a peace and an assurance we thought we would never lose. . . . The Apostle Paul [tried] to encourage new members who had just joined the Church, who undoubtedly had spiritual experiences and had received the pure light of testimony only to discover that not only had their troubles not ended, but that some of them had only begun. . . .
>
> . . . Don't distrust the experience you had. . . .
>
> . . . It certainly happens in matters of love and marriage. . . . I would like to have a dollar for every person in a courtship who knew he or she had felt the guidance of the Lord in that relationship, had prayed about the experience enough to know it was the will of the Lord, knew they loved each other and enjoyed each other's company, and saw a lifetime of wonderful compatibility ahead—only to panic, to get a brain cramp, to have total catatonic fear sweep over them. They "draw back," as Paul said, if not into perdition at least into marital paralysis.
>
> . . . *Remember the real thing*. . . . The light will again come. . . .
>
> . . . In the process of revelation and in making important decisions, fear almost always plays a destructive, sometimes paralyzing, role. . . .
>
> . . . *Along with the illuminating revelation that points us toward a righteous purpose or duty, God will also provide the means and power to achieve that purpose.* Trust in that eternal truth. If God has told you something is right, if something is indeed true for you, *he will provide*

> *the way for you to accomplish it.* That is true of joining the Church. It is true of getting an education, of going on a mission or of getting married or of any of a hundred worthy tasks. . . .
>
> . . . I believe that in our own individual ways, God takes us to the grove or the mountain or the temple and there shows us the wonder of what his plan is for us. . . . The adversary and his pinched, calculating little minions try to oppose such experiences and then try to darken them after the fact. But that is not the way of the gospel. That is not the way of a Latter-day Saint who claims as the fundamental fact of the Restoration the spirit of revelation.
>
> Fighting through darkness and despair and pleading for the light is what opened this dispensation. It is what keeps it going and it is what will keep you going. . . .
>
> *Cast not away therefore your confidence, which hath great recompence of reward.*
>
> *For if ye have need of patience, that after ye have done the will of God ye might receive the promise.* (Hebrews 10:35–36)[111]

In those times where we experience opposition after we have had revelation, we might ask the following questions to see whether we will "cast not away our confidence":

- Am I prepared for the opposition that will come?
- Will I hold on until the moment of greatest alarm?
- Will any persecution destroy the reality of the answers that God has given me?
- Am I more afraid of offending God or man? (see Joseph Smith—History 1:16, 24–25)[112]

---

111 Jeffrey R. Holland, "Cast Not Away Therefore Your Confidence," *BYU Speeches*, March 2, 1999.

112 S. Michael Wilcox, "What We Learn from Joseph Smith—History about Revelation."

The Grove of Trees that Becomes Sacred

Path leading into the Sacred Grove. The grove is filled with trails that allow solitude to allow visitors to reflect and feel the spirit of the grove. Photo by Casey Paul Griffiths.

The First Vision took place as the Joseph Smith Sr. family was making final arrangements to purchase their hundred-acre farm. The Sacred Grove is situated a quarter mile west of the Smiths' log home in Palmyra and the frame home on the Manchester farm. It is interesting that the "Sacred Grove is called 'one of the last surviving tracts of primeval forests in western New York state.'"[113] It is a ten-acre grove whose trees include maple, beech, hop hornbeam, wild cherry, ash, oak, hickory, and elm. There are still some trees in the grove today that date back to Joseph Smith's day. Of these trees, many are more than two hundred years old and reach almost a hundred feet in height.[114]

On December 26, 1905, in commemoration of Joseph Smith Jr.'s birthday, the prophet Joseph F. Smith, Joseph's nephew, visited the Smith farm and the Sacred Grove. There he met William A. Chapman, whose father, Seth T. Chapman, had purchased the farm on April 2, 1860. Joseph F. Smith learned that the wood lot had been kept in its same state and that for more than seventy years, "no axe [had] been laid at the roots of [the] trees" except to remove dead or decaying timber. Mr. Chapman explained that

113 *Donald L. Enders, "The Sacred Grove," Ensign*, April 1990, 14–17.

114 Lamar C. Berrett and Larry C. Porter, *Sacred Places: A Comprehensive Guide to LDS Historical Sites New York and Palmyra* (Salt Lake City: Deseret Book, 2000), 206.

"this was the particular piece of wood in which Joseph Smith claimed to see a vision; and his father had never felt disposed to mar its sacred silence or beauty."[115]

The Sacred Grove is still home to wildlife, such as this baby owl. Photo by Taylor Riley.

When the Sacred Grove was purchased by The Church of Jesus Christ of Latter-day Saints in the early 1900s, pilgrimages to this grove of trees became a sacred experience for many Latter-day Saints. No one knew the exact spot in the grove where the vision occurred—or even if the trees left standing when the grove was purchased were in the same part of the original grove where Joseph went to pray—but none of that was important. The grove became the visible symbol of the theophany that inaugurated the restoration of all things, and from it, the visiting Latter-day Saints would also gain spiritual sustenance and greater faith in the reality of the vision itself.[116]

Belief in the First Vision became a fundamental part of each Latter-day Saint's faith. In 1938, J. Reuben Clark Jr., in his seminal talk "The Charted Course of the Church in Education," told Latter-day Saint teachers that "the second of two things to which we must give full faith is that the Father and the Son actually and in truth and very deed appeared to the Prophet Joseph Smith in a vision in the woods. . . . together with all things necessarily implied therein or flowing therefrom." The reality of the vision was at

115 *Enders,* "Sacred Grove," 16.

116 T. Edgar Lyon, "How Authentic are Mormon Historic Sites in Vermont and New York?" *BYU Studies* 9, no. 3 (Spring 1969): 343–45.

the center of the whole concept of the Restoration, and, declared President Clark, "No teacher who does not have a real testimony of the . . . divine mission of Joseph Smith—including, in all its reality, the First Vision—has any place in the Church school system."[117] Then, in 1973, Elder Robert L. Simpson added, "The First Vision is the very foundation of this Church, and it is my conviction that each member of this Church performs his duty in direct ratio to his personal testimony and faith in the First Vision."[118] Having a testimony of the First Vision is a fundamental part of each Latter-day Saint's testimony of the Restoration of the gospel.

Mini-Devotional—Your Testimony of the First Vision

Next to the Atonement and Resurrection of Jesus Christ, nothing holds a more central place in the testimonies of Latter-day Saints than the sacred event of 1820 known as the First Vision. It is the key to the Restoration and will always be the key to everything that happens in our dispensation. Brigham Young disclosed that "no man or woman in this dispensation will ever enter into the celestial kingdom of God without the consent of Joseph Smith. From the day that the Priesthood was taken from the earth to the winding-up scene of all things, every man and woman must have the certificate of Joseph Smith, junior, as a passport of their entrance into the mansion where God and Christ are—I with you and you with me. I cannot go there without his consent."[119] The witness of Jesus Christ as the Savior and of Joseph Smith as the Prophet of Restoration is the foundation of all other appendages of a Latter-day Saint's testimony. We cannot believe in The Church of Jesus Christ of Latter-day Saints, we cannot believe in the Book of Mormon, we cannot believe that Christ restored his Church without also having a testimony of Joseph Smith.

- What is your testimony of the Prophet Joseph Smith?
- How did you receive your testimony of the First Vision?

117 J. Reuben Clark Jr., *The Charted Course of the Church in Education*, rev. ed. (Salt Lake City: The Church of Jesus Christ of Latter-day Saints, 1994) 3, 7.

118 Robert L. Simpson, "Our Fundamental Obligation: The Priesthood," *Conference Report*, October 1973, 102.

119 Brigham Young, "Intelligence, etc.," in *Journal of Discourses* (Liverpool, 1860), 7:289,https://contentdm.lib.byu.edu/digital/collection/JournalOfDiscourses3/id/2855.

Significant events at this location:

- Moroni, the final author and compiler of the Book of Mormon, buried the gold plates in this hill around AD 421.
- On the night of September 21, 1823, Moroni, now a glorified, resurrected being, visited Joseph Smith and told him about a hill near Joseph's house where the gold plates were buried.
- At Moroni's direction, Joseph Smith went to the hill on September 22, 1823, and found the plates, but Moroni told him that he must wait to receive them.
- Joseph Smith met Moroni at the Hill Cumorah on September 22 every year from 1824 to 1827.
- On September 22, 1827, Joseph went to the hill with his wife, Emma, to retrieve the plates.The plates were delivered up to the angel Moroni some time after Joseph Smith finished translating the Book of Mormon.
- The Church of Jesus Christ of Latter-day Saints purchased the entirety of the Hill Cumorah in 1928.
- The Hill Cumorah Pageant was held from 1917 to 2019.
- The Palmyra New York Temple was dedicated on April 6, 2000.

The Hill Cumorah

Monument to the Angel Moroni on the Hill Cumorah. Photo by Darren Gerber.

The Lord selected the Hill Cumorah as a sacred place since the time the Book of Mormon. Mormon and his son Moroni are the only Book of Mormon authors to use that particular name. Mormon uses *Cumorah* eight times (see Mormon 6:2–11), whereas Moroni only mentions *Cumorah* once (see Mormon 8:2). In the Book of Mormon, the word *Cumorah* is always in association with the final battle of the Nephite nation. Mormon and his soldiers marched "to the Land of Cumorah" and pitched their tents "round about the hill Cumorah" (Mormon 6:4). Mormon included that he hid records in the hill Cumorah, except for the few plates that he gave to Moroni (Mormon 6:6).

It is difficult to determine when the hill in Manchester, New York, was first called Cumorah during Joseph Smith's era. In the Doctrine and Covenants, the word *Cumorah* appears only once: "And again, what do we hear? Glad tidings from Cumorah!" (Doctrine and Covenants 128:20). Other than this reference, there are no other recorded instances of Joseph using the word *Cumorah* or instances where he is quoted identifying the hill.[120]

However, David Whitmer and Oliver Cowdery had a very interesting experience, which took place around June 1829. David recalled,

> A very pleasant, nice-looking old man suddenly appeared by the side of our wagon who saluted us with, "Good morning, it is very warm," at the same time wiping his face or forehead with his hand. We returned the salutation, and, by a sign from Joseph, I invited him to ride, if he were going our way. But he said very pleasantly, "No, I am going to Cumorah." This was something new to me, I did not know what Cumorah meant. We all gazed at him and at each other, and as I looked around inquiringly of Joseph, the old man instantly disappeared, so that I did not see him again. He had on his back a sort of knapsack with something that looked like a book. Joseph said: It was the messenger who had the plates who had taken them from Joseph just prior to our starting from Harmony.[121]

When preaching to the Delaware Indians in 1830, Oliver declared that the Book of Mormon "was hid in the earth by Moroni in a hill called by him, Cumorah, which hill is now in the state of New York, near the village of Palmyra."[122] In 1835, Edward Partridge also mentioned the hill by name in his journal: "We passed by the Hill Cumorah about 3 miles south

120 Rex C. Reeve and Richard O. Cowan, "The Hill Called Cumorah," in *Regional Studies in LDS Church History: New York*, ed. Larry C. Porter, Milton V. Backman Jr., and Susan Easton Black (Provo, UT; Brigham Young University Department of Church History and Doctrine, 1993), 73.

121 "Report of Elders Orson Pratt and Joseph F. Smith," *Deseret Evening News*, November 27, 1878, 2.

122 *Autobiography of Parley P. Pratt*, ed. Parley P. Pratt Jr. (Salt Lake City: Deseret Book Co., 1966), 55–56.

of Palmyra."[123] Among Latter-day Saints, identifying the hill as Cumorah was common, at least by 1835. However, in 1898, the US Geological Survey identified the hill simply as "the Mormon hill." But by 1952, the name on the map was changed to "Hill Cumorah."[124]

First Vision to the Hill Cumorah

Panorama of the Hill Cumorah. Photo by Casey Paul Griffiths.

On the night of September 21, 1823, Moroni, now a glorified, resurrected being, visited Joseph Smith in answer to his prayer. Moroni told Joseph about a hidden record of ancient peoples written on gold plates. As he related this information, Joseph was shown a vision of where the plates were buried in a hill near his father's farm. Joseph said, "Owing to the distinctness of the vision which I had had concerning it, I knew the place the instant I arrived there. . . . On the west side of this hill, not far from the top, under a stone of considerable size, lay the plates, deposited in a stone box" (Joseph Smith—History 1:50–51).

The next day, Joseph walked to the hill shown to him in the vision. Oliver Cowdery explained what Joseph experienced as he headed towards the hill:

> It seemed as though two invisible powers were influencing or striving to influence his mind—one with the reflection that if he obtained the object of his pursuit, it would be through the mercy and condescension of the Lord, and that every act or performance in relation to it, must be in strict accordance with the instruction of that personage, who

123 "The Journal of Bishop Edward Partridge," *Partridge-Young Family History Resource Page*, http://partridge.parkinsonfamily.org/histories/edward-journal.keys.htm.

124 Reeve and Cowan, "The Hill Called Cumorah," 74.

> communicated the intelligence to him first; and the other with the tho'ts [thoughts] and reflections like those previously mentioned—contrasting his former and present circumstances in life with those to come. That precious instruction recorded on the sacred page—pray always—which was expressly impressed upon him, was at length entirely forgotten, and . . . a fixed determination to obtain and aggrandize himself, occupied his mind when he arrived at the place where the record was found.[125]

Joseph explained what he found that day on the hill:

> Convenient to the village of Manchester, Ontario County, New York, stands a hill of considerable size, and the most elevated of any in the neighborhood. On the west side of this hill, not far from the top, under a stone of considerable size, lay the plates, deposited in a stone box. This stone was thick and rounding in the middle on the upper side, and thinner towards the edges, so that the middle part of it was visible above the ground, but the edge all around was covered with earth.
>
> Having removed the earth, I obtained a lever, which I got fixed under the edge of the stone, and with a little exertion raised it up. I looked in, and there indeed did I behold the plates, the Urim and Thummim, and the breastplate, as stated by the messenger. The box in which they lay was formed by laying stones together in some kind of cement. In the bottom of the box were laid two stones crossways of the box, and on these stones lay the plates and the other things with them. (Joseph Smith—History 1:51–52)

After removing the stone, Joseph tried to take the plates from the stone box three times, but each attempt resulted in a shock which caused him to stop. Each time, the shocks became more intense, and he finally exclaimed in frustration, "Why can I not obtain this book?"[126]

For the fifth time in twenty-four hours, the angel Moroni appeared, and he answered Joseph's question: "Because you have not kept the commandments of the Lord." Oliver Cowdery recorded that "in an instant all the former instructions, the great intelligence concerning Israel and the last

---

125 Joseph Smith History, 1834–1836, p. 85, The Joseph Smith Papers, accessed June 9, 2022, https://www.josephsmithpapers.org/paper-summary/history-1834-1836/89.

126 Joseph Smith History, 1834–1836, p. 94, The Joseph Smith Papers, accessed June 30, 2022, https://www.josephsmithpapers.org/paper-summary/history-1834-1836/98.

days, were brought to [Joseph's] mind. . . . but he had failed to remember the great end for which they [the gold plates] had been kept and in consequence could not have power to take them into his possession and bear them away."[127]

As Joseph proceeded to pray, "the glory of the Lord shone round about and rested upon him." As he gazed admiringly, the scene was abruptly changed from glorious light to the depths of darkness as he "beheld the prince of darkness, surrounded by his innumerable train of associates."[128] Moroni then explained this vision, a lesson in contrasts:

> All this is shown, the good and the evil, the holy and impure, the glory of God and the power of darkness, that you may know hereafter the two powers and never be influenced or overcome by that wicked one Behold, whatever entices and leads to good and to do good, is of God, and whatever does not is of that wicked one, It is he that fills the hearts of men with evil, to walk in darkness and blaspheme God; and you may learn from henceforth, that his ways are to destruction, but the way of holiness is peace and rest.[129]

Joseph explained that Moroni then informed him "that the time for bringing them [the plates] forth had not yet arrived, neither would it, until four years from that time; but he told me that I should come to that place precisely in one year from that time, and that he would there meet with me, and that I should continue to do so until the time should come for obtaining the plates" (Joseph Smith—History 1:53).

Joseph was instructed that he should return to the hill one year later when Moroni would again meet him and give him further instructions of "what the Lord was going to do, and how and in what manner his kingdom was to be conducted in the last days" (Joseph Smith—History 1:54).

127 Joseph Smith History, 1834–1836, p. 94–95, JSP.
128 Joseph Smith History, 1834–1836, p. 95, JSP.
129 Joseph Smith History, 1834–1836, p. 95, JSP.

Mini-Devotional—What Commandment Did Joseph Break?

During their first meeting the night of September 21, 1823, the angel Moroni gave Joseph Smith two commandments. The first commandment was to go to the hill where the plates were buried, which we now call Cumorah, the next morning. Joseph seemed to have kept this commandment perfectly. The second commandment was not to have any other motive in obtaining the gold plates than to build the kingdom. As Joseph went to the Hill Cumorah on September 22, 1823, we know that his motive was not singular. He did think about the monetary value of the gold plates. However, his motives were not selfish: he was worried about the financial plight of his family, and he wanted to help them. While he had a good motive, it was not the right one. Motive is important in the things we do—for Joseph Smith and for us.

- Why is it important to have building the kingdom as our primary motivation?
- Have there been times in your life when you were motivated by more than one thing and did something good for the wrong motivation?
- Have you ever been 100 percent motivated to just build the kingdom?
- Why is it important to be motivated by the right reason?

Appearances of the Angel Moroni on September 22, 1824–1827

Detail of the Angel Moroni monument on the Hill Cumorah. Photo by Casey Paul Griffiths.

When September 22, 1824, arrived, Joseph Smith returned to Cumorah's hillside, thinking, once again, that he would receive the gold plates.[130] As before, Joseph dislodged the stone lid and looked upon the sacred contents of the cement box. But this time, as he did, he wondered if there might be anything else in the box that might be of temporal worth. Laying the plates upon the ground, he checked the box, hoping to find additional treasure, but he found nothing. He then replaced the stone, covering it up, so there would be no indication that the ground had been disturbed. However, when he turned around and reached for the plates, they were gone! In alarm, he knelt, asking the Lord why the plates had been taken. Moroni instantly appeared, reminding him that he had not done as he had been commanded. According to his mother, Joseph "had been commanded, not to lay the plates down, or put them for a moment out of his hands, until he got to the house and deposited them in a chest or trunk, with a good lock and key."[131]

Joseph must have been greatly relieved when Moroni instructed him to again dislodge the stone cover and see that the gold plates were safely in place. However, when he reached to get them once again "he was hurled back upon the ground with great violence" which must have caused him to

130 Lucy Mack Smith, History, 1845, p. 87, JSP.
131 Lucy Mack Smith, History, 1845, p. 88, JSP.

be unconscious for a few moments.[132] For when he recovered, he found that he was once again alone. Joseph returned home "weeping with grief and disappointment."[133] Expecting to receive the plates, he was fearful his family might question his story since they had the same expectation; however, when he related to his family what had happened, they believed him. His mother wrote: "We therefore doubled our dilligence in prayer and supplication to God, in order that he might be more fully instructed in his duty, and be preserved from all the wiles and machinations of him 'who lieth in wait to deceive.'"[134]

As Joseph then recounted, "Accordingly, as I had been commanded, I went at the end of each year, and at each time I found the same messenger there and received instructions and intelligence from him at each of our interviews, respecting what the Lord was going to do, and how and in what manner his kingdom was to be conducted in the last days" (Joseph Smith—History 1:54). Joseph was allowed to share with his family the instructions he had received from Moroni; however, he was forbidden to share them with anyone else, maybe to prevent the persecution that was gathering around the young Prophet. Joseph was adept at describing what took place each time. His mother reported, "During our evening conversations, Joseph would occasionally give us some of the most amusing recitals that could be imagined: he would describe the ancient inhabitants of this continent; their dress, mode of travelling, and the animals upon which they rode; their cities, and their buildings, with every particular; he would describe their <mode of> warfare, as also their religious worship. This he would do with as much ease, seemingly, as if he had spent his whole life with them."[135]

It seems that the angelic instructions were not limited to that September night. One time early in the year of 1827, Joseph went to Manchester and returned later than expected. His family was somewhat worried when he did not return on time. When he arrived, his father inquired whether he had had any trouble. Joseph "smiled, and said in a calm tone, 'I have taken

132 Lucy Mack Smith, History, 1845, p. 88, JSP.

133 Lucy Mack Smith, History, 1845, p. 88, JSP.

134 Lucy Mack Smith, History, 1845, p. 88–89, JSP.

135 Lucy Mack Smith, History, 1845, p. 87, The Joseph Smith Papers, accessed June 30, 2022, https://www.josephsmithpapers.org/paper-summary/lucy-mack-smith-history-1845/94.

the severest chastisement that I have ever had in my life.'"[136] Learning of that, his father was angry, supposing that some malicious neighbor had mistreated his son, but then Joseph explained:

> Stop, father, Stop. . . . It was an angel of the Lord—as I passed by the hill of Cumorah, where the plates are, the angel met me and said, that I had not been engaged enough in the work of the Lord; that the time had come for the Record to <be> brought forth; and, that I must be up and doing, and set myself about the things which God had commanded me to do: but Father, . . . give yourself no uneasiness concerning the reprimand that I have received; for I now know the course that I am to pursue; so all will be well.[137]

Mini-Devotional—Weakness of Youth

Joseph Smith talked about his experiences as a teenager while he was waiting to acquire the gold plates:

> I was left to all kinds of temptations; and mingling with all kinds of society, I frequently fell into many foolish errors, and displayed the weakness of youth, and the foibles of human nature; which, I am sorry to say, led me into divers temptations, offensive in the sight of God. In making this confession, no one need suppose me guilty of any great or malignant sins. A disposition to commit such was never in my nature. But I was guilty of levity, and sometimes associated with jovial company, etc., not consistent with that character which ought to be maintained by one who was called of God as I had been. But this will not seem very strange to anyone who recollects my youth and is acquainted with my native cheery temperament. (Joseph Smith—History 1:28)

You might notice that Joseph spoke of the weakness of youth (singular) rather than the weaknesses of youth (plural). Some of us still struggle with the weakness of youth or inexperience. As Joseph recounted his temptations

136 Lucy Mack Smith, History, 1845, p. 104, The Joseph Smith Papers, accessed June 30, 2022, https://www.josephsmithpapers.org/paper-summary/lucy-mack-smith-history-1845/111.

137 Lucy Mack Smith, History, 1845, p. 104, JSP.

during this time, he was not speaking of "great or malignant sins"; rather, he called them "foibles of human nature and foolish errors." Joseph never had the disposition to commit sin, but he was tempted with making errors or mistakes. Joseph's temptations might have included such matters as fixating on an idea, failing to discern between the Spirit of God and the adversary, treating things with levity, or choosing the wrong friends.

- What temptations in the weakness of youth are/were you tempted with?
- What foibles of human nature or foolish errors have you been tempted with?
- Have you, like Joseph, been of the disposition to never commit such sins?

Joseph was a happy individual and felt that he had a "native cheery temperament"; however, at the same time, he felt he was "guilty of levity." Speaking of his friends, he said that he "sometimes associated with jovial company, etc., not consistent with that character which ought to be maintained by one who was called of God as [he] had been."

- What is the difference between cheerfulness and levity?
- Do you ever associate with jovial company not consistent with your callings?

Joseph seemed to be struggling with the dichotomy of wanting to have fun and wanting to have his actions be consistent with his calling as a prophet. Joseph was not saying he was not serious enough. The Lord does not want us to be dour and serious all the time. Rather, Joseph was learning the difference between being lighthearted and light-minded.

- What is the difference between being lighthearted and light-minded?

Joseph Receives the Gold Plates

Hiking trails on the Hill Cumorah. Photo by Casey Paul Griffiths.

On September 22, 1827, Joseph Smith took Emma Hale Smith, his young bride of eight months, with him to the Hill Cumorah. In an account written by Joseph Knight, Sr. as well as a separate by the Prophet's sister Katherine Smith, it is recorded that the young Prophet was told in 1823 that he could have the gold plates the next year if he brought the right person. When Joseph asked who the right person was, the answer was, "Your oldest brother," Alvin Smith. Alvin always showed the most intense interest and was always Joseph's greatest ally in his ventures with the angel Moroni. But before September 1824 came, Alvin had died.[138]

So, Joseph Smith went to the hill alone. Joseph Knight reported that in 1825, Joseph was told he could have the plates the next year, like before, if he brought the right person. This time when Joseph asked who the right

138 William G. Hartley, *Stand by My Servant Joseph: The Story of the Joseph Knight Family and the Restoration* (Salt Lake City: Deseret Book, 2003), 26.

person was, the answer was, "You will know." Joseph looked in his seer stone and found that the right person was Emma.[139]

Lucy Mack Smith was up late on the night of September 21, 1827, taking care of some household chores. Joseph came to her around midnight, asking if she had a chest with a lock and key. She told him that she did not, but Joseph assured her that it was fine.[140] Joseph and Emma then left for Cumorah in a horse-drawn wagon. Emma recounted that she waited at the bottom of the hill as Joseph climbed up the hill in the dark.

The young couple did not return to the Smith home until midmorning. Little is known of what happened in those eight to ten hours after Joseph finally received the plates. He simply recorded:

> At length the time arrived for obtaining the plates, the Urim and Thummim, and the breastplate. On the twenty-second day of September, one thousand eight hundred and twenty-seven, having gone as usual at the end of another year to the place where they were deposited, the same heavenly messenger delivered them up to me with this charge: that I should be responsible for them; that if I should let them go carelessly, or through any neglect of mine, I should be cut off; but that if I would use all my endeavors to preserve them, until he, the messenger, should call for them, they should be protected. (Joseph Smith—History 1:59)

It was soon known abroad that Joseph had the gold plates, and "the most strenuous exertions were used to get them" from him.[141] Joseph said, "The persecution became more bitter and more severe than before, and multitudes were on the alert continually to get them from me if possible" (Joseph Smith—History 1:60).

---

139 Hartley, *Stand by My Servant Joseph*, 26.

140 Lucy Mack Smith, History, 1845, p. 105, JSP.

141 H. Donl Peterson, "Moroni: Joseph Smith's Teacher," in *Regional Studies in Latter-day Saint Church History: New York*, ed. Larry C. Porter, Milton V. Backman Jr., Susan Easton Black (Provo, UT: Brigham Young University Department of Church History and Doctrine, 1992), 57.

Mini-Devotional—Discerning Voices

Through his experiences at the Hill Cumorah, Joseph learned to discern different voices. Joseph's first lesson was to discern the difference between the Spirit of God and the spirit of the adversary. His second lesson was to discern between the voice of the Spirit and his own thoughts. The third lesson was to listen to the voice of God over the voice of his friends or the voice of man. As a young prophet, Joseph had to learn early on how to distinguish these many voices. We, too, need to learn these same lessons of discerning.

- How can we learn to discern between the voice of the Spirit of God and the spirit of the adversary?
- Have you had experiences where you were able to discern between the voice of the Lord and your own thoughts?

The Gold Plates Are Returned to the Angel Moroni and Cumorah's Cave

A stone on the Hill Cumorah. Photo by Kenneth Mays.

Joseph Smith recorded what happened to the plates after he had finished translating them: "When, according to arrangements, the messenger called for them [the gold plates], I delivered them up to him; and he has them in his charge until this day, being the second day of May, one thousand eight hundred and thirty-eight" (Joseph Smith—History 1:60). But how—and where—did this transaction happen?

Many of Joseph's associates have told of a cave within the Hill Cumorah where Joseph, along with Oliver Cowdery, delivered the plates when they had finished translating them.[142] Brigham Young gave multiple descriptions of a cave within the Hill Cumorah. In 1877, Brigham recounted: "The angel instructed him [Joseph] to carry the plates back to the hill Cumorah,

142 Cameron J. Packer, "Cumorah's Cave," *Journal of Book of Mormon Studies* 13, no. 1 (2004): 52.

which he did. Oliver said that when Joseph and Oliver got there, the hill opened up, and they walked into a cave, in which there was a large and spacious room. . . . They laid the plates on a table; it was a large table that stood in the room."[143] In a discourse in 1855, W. W. Phelps related a story told to him by Hyrum Smith where Hyrum, along with Joseph and Oliver, "went to the hill Cormorah [*sic*]. As they were walking up the hill, a door opened, and they walked into a room about 16 ft. square."[144]

Beyond the physical description of the cave, many accounts report on the contents stored in the room. Orson Pratt wrote of a "grand repository of all the numerous records of the ancient nations of the western continent" that was "located in another department of the hill [Cumorah]."[145] Brigham Young noted that there was a table in the room and that "under this table there was a pile of plates as much as two feet high, and there were altogether in this room more plates than probably many wagon loads; they were piled up in the corners and along the walls." Other accounts mention boxes of treasure, sacred implements, arms, and precious metals and stones.[146]

Brigham also spoke of the sword of Laban being in the room: "The first time they [Oliver and Joseph] went there the sword of Laban hung upon the wall; but when they went again it had been taken down and laid upon the table across the gold plates; it was unsheathed, and on it was written these words: 'This sword will never be sheathed again until the kingdoms of this world become the kingdom of our God and his Christ.'"[147] The contents and existence of the cave in the Hill Cumorah holds meaning in the continuing restoration of God's kingdom on earth: The sword is still unsheathed. There is more for God to reveal.

143 Brigham Young, "Trying to Be Saints—Treasures of the Everlasting Hills—the Hill Cumorah—Obedience to True Principle the Key to Knowledge—All Enjoyment Comes from God—Organization—Duties of Officers—Final Results," in *Journal of Discourses* (Liverpool, 1878), 19:38, https://contentdm.lib.byu.edu/digital/collection/JournalOfDiscourses3/id/1105.

144 William Horne Dame, *Journal of the Southern Exploring Company*, 1854–1858, Iron County, UT, January 14, 1855, Della Edwards Papers, Special Collections, J. Willard Marriot Library, University of Utah.

145 Packer, "Cumorah's Cave," 55.

146 Packer, "Cumorah's Cave," 54.

147 Brigham Young, "Trying to Be Saints," 38.

The Church of Jesus Christ of Latter-day Saints Purchases the Hill Cumorah

The Hill Cumorah with many of its trees removed in the early 20th Century. Photo courtesy Church History Library.

During the last half of the nineteenth century, many Latter-day Saints, missionaries serving in the eastern states, and General Authorities occasionally visited the Hill Cumorah, but persecution and poverty prevented the Church from actually purchasing the property.[148] Because the Church did not own the Hill Cumorah, Latter-day Saints who wished to visit the hill encountered problems. Willard Bean, who took over ownership of Joseph Smith Farm in 1914, remarked: "They used to drive our visitors off the hill. And the tenants would not allow us to park a car on or near the Hill Cumorah."[149]

---

148 Reeve and Cowan, "The Hill Called Cumorah," 74.

149 "Autobiography of Willard Washington Bean: Exploits of the Fighting Parson 1868–1949," Willard Washington Bean Autobiography, Vault MSS SC 1529, L. Tom Perry Special Collections, Harold B. Lee Library, Brigham Young University, Provo, UT, 241–43.

The hill, as well as several surrounding farms, was owned by Pliny T. Sexton, a wealthy banker in Palmyra in the early 1900s. On one occasion, President Heber J. Grant and Presiding Bishop Charles W. Nibley met with Pliny at his bank, and Bishop Nibley made the following suggestion: "Mr. Sexton, this has been a most pleasant visit. We have enjoyed it immensely and now in order to make a perfect fay of it, let me phone up the morning newspaper in Rochester and have them send a photographer over with a movie camera and have you go down in history by having you photographed on top of Cumorah Hill in the act of handing the deed to that historic property to Heber J. Grant, president of the Mormon church."[150]

Pliny declined the offer, feeling he could take better advantage of the Church's interest and get a higher price for the property. Later, he offered to sell it for one hundred thousand dollars, but the Church declined his offer. Bishop Nibley later said, "When the Lord wants us to get possession of that Hill, the way will be opened up."[151]

Elder George Albert Smith of the Quorum of the Twelve Apostles was indispensable in obtaining the Hill Cumorah so Latter-day Saints could visit it unhindered. After fifteen years of married life, George Albert and wife, Lucy Smith, went on what they called a second honeymoon. Their chief destination was Palmyra, and they carried with them twenty thousand dollars—the money sewn into Lucy's skirt—for the purpose of buying the hill. When they arrived, George Albert called on Pliny, the owner of the hill, asking him to put a price on the Hill Cumorah. Pliny refused to do business in "any such hasty fashion," but he offered to take the Smiths on a tour of the hill the following day.[152] "On the tour, [Pliny] Sexton drove his visitors all over the countryside, but he still declined to put a price on the hill. George Albert spent a day in consultation with German E. Ellsworth and Ashby Snow, who were there to assist in the venture. They were especially eager to make a deal on the hill because a delegation from the Reorganized Church also seemed to be interested in purchasing it. Pliny saw the obvious advantage in letting the two groups bid against each other."[153]

Pliny died without selling any of his property to the Church. After his death, his niece headed a group of prejudiced heirs of estate who pledged

150 "Autobiography of Willard Washington Bean," 241.

151 "Autobiography of Willard Washington Bean," 242.

152 "Autobiography of Willard Washington Bean," 242.

153 Merlo J. Pusey, *Builder of the Kingdom: George A. Smith, John Henry Smith, George Albert Smith*, (Provo, UT: Brigham Young University Press, 1981), 243.

not to sell the Hill Cumorah for any price. Willard Bean reported that "they were sore because we refused to give the old gentleman Sexton a hundred thousand dollars for the Hill."[154] However, with time, and needing cash, the Sexton heirs eventually allowed the Hill Cumorah to be sold.

On February 2, 1928, Willard Bean sent a letter to the First Presidency telling them of the terms of the purchase he had received from the Sexton heirs. He received the following in reply: "Please secure a definite offer, in writing, if you can possibly do so, from the executors of Mr. Sexton's estate, for the Hill farm of 170 acres. If they will not sell it alone, get a definite offer on the other pieces of property with the Hill. But to make it binding, it would be best to have this offer in writing."[155] Willard was able to meet these requirements and purchase the hill.

In general conference of April 1928, Anthony W. Ivins, First Counselor in the First Presidency, said: "I thank God that in a way which seems to have been providential [the Hill Cumorah] has come into the possession of the Church."[156]

The Angel Moroni Monument, Bureau of Information, and Visitors' Center

The visitor's center at the Hill Cumorah. Photo by Kenneth Mays.

154 "Autobiography of Willard Washington Bean," 243.

155 Willard W. Bean, "Change of Sentiment." *Improvement Era*, June 1928, 686.

156 Anthony W. Ivins. *Conference Report*, April 1928, 15.

After the Church finally gained ownership of the Hill Cumorah, they began to make plans to construct a large monument to commemorate the visit of Moroni and to stand as a witness of the Restoration of the gospel of Jesus Christ. Sculptor Torleif S. Knaphus designed the monument to symbolize a pillar of light. Bronze-sculptured panels on the four faces of the monument's base feature Joseph Smith receiving the plates from Moroni (on the west), the angel showing the plates to the Three Witnesses (on the south), the Eight Witnesses seeing the plates (on the east), and Moroni's challenge to readers of the Book of Mormon (see Moroni 10:4).[157]

The dedication of the monument took place on July 21, 1935. The mayor of Palmyra attended the ceremony and apologized for the earlier prejudice that had taken place in his city. President Heber J. Grant personally dedicated the thirty-five-thousand-dollar monument. In his dedication, he stated:

> We are truly grateful unto thee, our Heavenly Father, for the hospitality of the people in this section of the country. We are grateful that the spirit of opposition has disappeared. We are thankful that the reputation of thy people has changed. . . . O Father, and in the name of our Redeemer we dedicate unto thee at this time, this monument that has been erected upon this sacred Hill. We dedicate the Hill itself in the ground surrounding it and all the materials that have been used in this monument and we humbly pray unto thee that it may be preserved from the elements that it may stand here as a testimony of God, of Jesus Christ, and of the dealings of Jesus Christ with the people that lived anciently upon this continent.[158]

President David O. McKay, Second Counselor in the First Presidency at the time, explained what was taking place at the dedication: "We are not erecting [the monument] to perpetuate the deeds of Moroni, nor are we erecting it to honor his father Mormon, nor indeed to perpetuate the life and deeds of Joseph Smith. This monument is built as an expression of gratitude for the restoration of the Gospel of Jesus Christ and as a manifestation

157 Allen P. Gerritsen, "The Hill Cumorah Monument: An Inspired Creation of Torleif S. Knaphus," *Journal of Book of Mormon Studies* 13, no. 1 (2004): 130.

158 Dedication of the Hill Cumorah Monument, July 21, 1935, Historical Department of The Church of Jesus Christ of Latter-day Saints, Salt Lake City.

to all the world of our faith in the personality and divine fatherhood of God."[159]

Because it had previously been stripped of trees, the Hill Cumorah was reforested with thirty-one thousand evergreen and hardwood seedlings between 1928 and 1929 under Willard Bean's direction. Other plantings also followed. In April 1976, the statue of Moroni was taken down, and its gold leaf was refurbished. It was replaced on the monument with its pedestal rotated ninety degrees from its original north-facing direction so that it faced the west.

On August 29, 1937, two years after the monument's dedication, the Bureau of Information was dedicated by Elder John A. Widtsoe of the Quorum of the Twelve Apostles.[160] Later renamed the Hill Cumorah Visitors' Center, it sits on the west side of the hill and was designed to resemble ancient American architecture.

The Hill Cumorah Pageant

The Hill Cumorah pageant was staged on this part of the hill for nearly ninety years. When the pageant ended in 2019 efforts began to fill in this portion of the hill with trees. Photo by Casey Paul Griffiths.

159 Dedication of the Hill Cumorah Monument.

160 Larry C. Porter, "Western New York," in *Sacred Places New York and Pennsylvania: A Comprehensive Guide to Early LDS Historical Sites*, ed. LaMar C. Berrett and Larry C. Porter (Salt Lake City: Deseret Book Co., 2000), 161.

For nearly a century, the production of the Hill Cumorah Pageant blessed the lives of thousands people and has taken its place among countless influential events in the history of The Church of Jesus Christ of Latter-day Saints. Though the pageant began in 1917, it was not until twenty years later that it became the esteemed production that lasted until 2019. A large portion of the pageant's success was the result of a single mission call: Harold I. Hansen was called to the Eastern States Mission in 1937 and was subsequently asked to direct a small play on the Hill Cumorah. The audience of that year's production included about fifteen thousand people, and only about a thousand were members of the Church.

Harold poured his heart and soul into the pageant for nearly forty years. Even as he was raising his family in Utah, he returned to New York every summer. Except for the years during World War II, which forced the pageant to shut down for six years, his unwavering effort year after year touched the lives of many participants, and the pageant itself became an important conversion opportunity for the many audience members.

In 1953, because of the Korean War, there was a limited number of missionary volunteers who could participate in the pageant. To solve this problem, Harold invited young adult women from the west, such as those who attended Brigham Young University in Utah, to join in the production. Hundreds of volunteers were selected, and then they all embarked on the four-day cross-country bus ride. When they arrived, they were asked to abide by missionary standards, including wearing mission attire and having a companion.The expectations put on the missionaries and other volunteers at the pageant allowed both the audience and participants to be moved by the Spirit.[161] Many participants expressed that the pageant played a significant role in the development of their testimony; some of them stated that it was the greatest spiritual experience of their lives. Additionally, many audience members expressed that the pageant was the "'push' they needed in making up their minds to join the Church."[162]

Backstage, many other volunteers were instrumental in helping the pageant run smoothly. Sister missionaries dedicated their time to sew new costumes. Later, when the production needed costumes for more than six

---

161 Mary Jane Woodger, "Harold and the Hill" in *Regional Studies in Latter-day Saint Church History New York-Pennsylvania*, ed. Alexander L. Baugh and Andrew H. Hedges, (Provo, Utah: Brigham Young University Department of Church History and Doctrine, 2002), 155–64.

162 Woodger, "Harold and the Hill," 158–59.

hundred characters and actors, members of Relief Societies in the area also sacrificed their time to provide the costumes.[163]

Surprisingly, summer rainstorms also helped to build the testimonies of participants and audience members. There were many instances when rain was forecasted during the productions but miraculously ceased for the performance. One newspaper headline read "Mormon Luck Prevails: Pageant Goes On" after a performance seemed to stop the rain completely. People eventually picked up on the pattern, which put a lot of pressure on Harold. During the few times that rain did cancel the production, Harold was relieved to be ridden of the expectation that the Lord would stop the rain.[164]

The pageant went through several changes over time. In 1953, Crawford Gates was asked to compose an original score for the pageant. Four years later, the Utah Symphony and representatives from three Brigham Young University choruses met to record the music. The score filled 284 pages and turned into one hour and seventeen minutes of recording. The recording process did not go smoothly at first. After three out of four sessions, only seven of nineteen movements had been recorded. This halting progress prompted Crawford to pray for a miracle. The fourth session began with a prayer, and the next five movements were recorded flawlessly the first time, despite groups only having had one rehearsal. The rest of the movements were recorded soon after. Miraculously, they finished recording in time for that year's pageant.

Crawford's musical score was used for nearly thirty years until Church leaders decided to improve the pageant based on feedback from nonmembers. Author Orson Scott Card was asked to write a new script for the pageant that would be easier for nonmembers to follow. Although Orson changed many aspects of the original script, the theme of Jesus Christ and his restored gospel remained. Crawford was then asked to compose a new musical score to reflect the changes in the script.[165] The decision to end the Hill Cumorah Pageant, despite its influence, was not easy for Church leadership. Elder D. Todd Christofferson explained the decision at a devotional celebrating the pageant in 2021:

---

163 Gerald S. Argetsinger, "The Hill Cumorah Pageant: A Historical Perspective," *Journal of Book of Mormon Studies* 13, no. 1 (2004): 62.

164 Woodger, "Harold and the Hill," 162–68.

165 Reeve and Cowan, "The Hill Called Cumorah," 85–88.

> We are now at a time in the history of the Church when the vast majority of its members will never see the Hill Cumorah or visit the Sacred Grove. The fame of these places will endure and grow, but relatively few will ever be there. The First Presidency determined that in what is increasingly a truly worldwide Church, we could not justify the cost of present and future maintenance, security and safety upgrades, and ongoing operations running into several million dollars in just the near term when only a relative handful of members and visitors will ever benefit from the experience. . . . Yes, the Hill Cumorah Pageant was a formative experience for many of us, but going forward, different and equally compelling formative experiences will come for families and for the current and future rising generations. Those experiences will be tailored to their time and suited to their need.[166]

Though future generations in the Church will never have the opportunity to see the Hill Cumorah Pageant in person, the 2019 production is available on the Church's website for all who wish to see it.[167] The pageant's legacy will continue despite its discontinuance, living on in the hearts of its participants and audiences, no matter whether the audience saw it live or via the 2019 recording. The Hill Cumorah Pageant is a masterpiece of cooperation and artistic skill, and the members of the pageant that labored with love will be forever remembered for their participation in this great demonstration of faith in Christ's restored Church.

Mini-Devotional—Trusting in His Timing

When Elder D. Todd Christofferson was a young man performing in the Hill Cumorah Pageant, he went to the Sacred Grove alone to pray for the same things that Joseph Smith had prayed for in 1820. When he did not receive an answer, he left disappointed. Weeks later, while studying the Book of Mormon in his basement bedroom of his parents' home in New Jersey, he received confirmation of the truthfulness of the gospel. He realized that "you cannot tell God how and when He should respond to your

166 D. Todd Christofferson, *Hill Cumorah Pageant Commemorative Devotional*, July 9, 2021, The Church of Jesus Christ of Latter-day Saints.

167 "The Hill Cumorah Pageant," The Church of Jesus Christ of Latter-day Saints, https://www.churchofjesuschrist.org/media/video/2021-06-1000-hill-cumorah-pageant.

prayers. You have to say, 'I am always open. I am always ready. I am always willing to hear.'"[168]

- What can we do to ensure that we are always ready to hear God's voice?
- When have you received answers to your prayers?
- How in your life has the Lord's timing worked in better ways than you could have imagined?

The Palmyra New York Temple

The Palmyra New York temple can be seen through the trees from the Smith Family Farm. Photo by Casey Paul Griffiths.

The Palmyra New York Temple, the seventy-seventh temple of the Church, was built more than a century and a half after the Church's

168 D. Todd Christofferson, "I Hear Him through Prayer, Pondering, and Trusting in Him," The Church of Jesus Christ of Latter-day Saints, https://www.churchofjesuschrist.org/inspiration/i-hear-him-through-prayer-pondering-and-trusting-in-him?lang=eng

organization in the place where it all began—the "cradle of the Restoration."[169] The story of the Palmyra Temple is faith-building evidence that the Lord can work miracles in the lives of his servants. While restoring the Smith log home in Palmyra, the Church needed to purchase a one-acre plot of land directly to the east of the home. The owner of that land, Ted Bellefontaine, had a tight grip on the property and agreed to sell the land only if the Church would build a house for him on a spot of his choosing. The Church agreed to his terms and built the house. Tragically, Ted was killed in a snowmobile accident before he had the chance to occupy his new home. Later, President Gordon B. Hinckley designated the spot where the house had been built for the Palmyra Temple, and the house was relocated.[170]

In 1996, President Hinckley made a goal to have one hundred temples in operation before the year 2000. This goal opened the door for smaller temples to be built, including the Palmyra Temple, which was officially announced on February 9, 1999. A few months later on May 25, Church leaders conducted the groundbreaking ceremony, and in March 2000, the temple was completed and several open houses were held.

169 Veneese C. Nelson, "The Palmyra Temple: A Significant Link to LDS Church History," in *Regional Studies in Latter-day Saint Church History New York-Pennsylvania*, ed. Alexander L. Baugh and Andrew H. Hedges, (Provo, Utah: Brigham Young University Department of Church History and Doctrine, 2002), 148.

170 Nelson, "The Palmyra Temple," 224–28.

The window of the Palmyra Temple facing the Smith Farm was made of clear rather than stained glass so that temple patrons could see the Sacred Grove from the Temple. Photo by Casey Paul Griffiths.

On April 6, 2000—the 170th anniversary of the organization of the Church—President Hinckley dedicated the Palmyra Temple. It rained that day, but when President Hinckley went outside to perform the cornerstone ceremony, the rain stopped, and the sun shone—a miracle in his eyes. He proclaimed, "There will never be another day quite like this in the history of this work where we will dedicate a sacred house in this historic and marvelous place."[171]

As with any construction project, there were disruptions, but the Lord blessed those that worked on the Palmyra Temple. One such blessing involved the stained-glass windows of the temple. The windows that were initially proposed for the temple were going to be too expensive, but a donation covered the cost of the project. Creator Tom Holdman then crafted twenty-seven beautiful windows for the temple, some of which depict the Tree of Life and the First Vision. Such a project would have normally taken a year to complete, but Tom miraculously was able to complete the windows in four months.[172]

---

171 Carrie Moore, "LDS Temple Dedicated," *Deseret News*, April 6, 2000, https://www.deseret.com/2000/4/6/19556632/lds-temple-dedicated.

172 Nelson, "The Palmyra Temple," 227.

What a blessing it is to have a house of the Lord built in the vicinity of the Hill Cumorah, a place so dear to the hearts of members of The Church of Jesus Christ of Latter-day Saints. It is significant that the turn of the century welcomed this holy temple located at the origin of the Restoration.

Significant events at this location:

- This grave marker commemorates the life of Alvin Smith, the beloved older brother of the Prophet Joseph Smith.
- The Martin Harris farm is where the first portion of the Book of Mormon was taken in the summer of 1828 and where it was stolen.
- Martin Harris mortgaged his farm to pay for the printing of the Book of Mormon.

ALVIN SMITH'S GRAVE AND THE MARTIN HARRIS FARM

Headstone of Alvin Smith in the General John Swift Memorial Cemetery. Photo by Casey Paul Griffiths.

Alvin Smith's Grave

The grave marker for Alvin Smith is located in the General John Swift Memorial Cemetery, not far from Main Street in Palmyra. Visitors can park at the bottom of the hill and then proceed up a short staircase. The cemetery is located on the top of the hill, and Alvin's grave marker is not difficult to find. Alvin's original grave was washed away due to erosion. In the early twentieth century, the grave marker was found by Willard Bean and

Harold Stoner and placed at its current location. Because the grave marker was badly eroded, it was placed in a granite marker for its preservation.[173]

Alvin Smith was Joseph Smith's oldest brother and passed away on November 19, 1823. According to Lucy Mack Smith, Alvin became ill when a doctor gave him a dose of calomel, which lodged in Alvin's stomach and became gangrenous. After several days of immense pain, Alvin called together his siblings, providing each sibling with some final words of advice. When Alvin spoke to Joseph, Alvin said, "I want you to be a good boy, and do everything that lays in your power to obtain the record—be faithful in receiving instruction, and in keeping every commandment that is given you—your brother Alvin must leave now, but remember the example which he has set for you, and set the same example for the children that are younger than yourself—and always be kind to father and mother."[174]

Lucy Mack Smith, Alvin Smith's mother, recalled that it was painful to speak about the Book of Mormon for a time following Alvin's death because "Alvin had ever manifested a greater zeal and anxiety if it were possible than any of the rest of with regard to the record which had been shown to Joseph."[175] Her memory of Alvin's enthusiasm to assist Joseph in bringing forth the Book of Mormon is supported by several recollections from local friends and neighbors. Some of these recollections come from individuals who supported the Smiths and others from individuals who saw them as their enemies. Joseph Knight, a close family friend, recalled that an angel told Joseph Smith the angel would give Joseph Smith the record the next year when they met on September 23, if Joseph Smith brought Alvin with him.[176] During the ensuing year, Alvin died. Willard Chase, who was antagonistic toward the Smiths, said that the angel told Joseph, "Come one year from this day, and bring with you your eldest brother, and you shall have them . . . but before the expiration of the year, his oldest brother died."[177] According to Joseph Knight, after Alvin's death the angel instead

173 Kenneth Mays, "Portraits of the Past: Alvin Smith's Grave," Deseret News, March 31, 2011, https://www.deseret.com/2011/3/31/20385194/portraits-of-the-past-alvin-smith-s-grave.

174 Lucy Mack Smith, History, 1845, p. 91, The Joseph Smith Papers.

175 Lucy Mack Smith, History, 1844–1845, bk. 4, [7], p. 49,; see also Kyle R. Walker, *United by Faith: The Joseph Sr. and Lucy Mack Smith Family* (American Fork, UT: Covenant Communications, Inc., 2005), 83.

176 Dean Jessee, "Joseph Knight's Recollection of Early Mormon History," *BYU Studies* 17, no. 1 (Autumn 1976): 3–4.

177 Quoted in Walker, *United by Faith*, 104.

instructed Joseph Smith to bring Emma Hale with him to the hill. Emma was present at the bottom of the hill the night Joseph received the plates on September 23, 1827.[178]

The Alvin Smith monument was placed in this more durable granite monument. Photo by Casey Paul Griffiths.

The family's grief was further added to at Alvin Smith's funeral. Even though Mother Smith characterized Alvin as a man "of singular goodness of disposition,"[179] the clergyman preaching the funeral sermon condemned Alvin for being unbaptized. William Smith, Alvin's youngest brother, reported, "Rev. Stockton had preached at my brother's funeral sermon and intimated very strongly that he had gone to hell, for Alvin was not a church member, but he was a good boy and my father did not like it."[180]

Compounding the pain surrounding Alvin Smith's death, rumors apparently began to circulate around Palmyra that Alvin's body was removed from its grave for unknown purposes. Nearly a year after Alvin's death, Joseph Smith Sr. ran a public notice six times in a Palmyra newspaper,

178 Jessee, "Joseph Knight's Recollection of Early Mormon History," 4.

179 Lucy Mack Smith, History, 1844–1845, bk. 4, [5], JSP.

180 Quoted Walker, *United by Faith*, 100.

hoping to quell the vicious rumors surrounding Alvin's body. Father Smith's notice read as follows:

> TO THE PUBLIC: Whereas reports have been industriously put in circulation that my son Alvin had been removed from the place of his interment and dissected; . . . therefore, for the purpose of ascertaining the truth of such reports, I, with some of my neighbors this morning, repaired to the grave, and removing the earth, found the body, which had not been disturbed. This method is taken for the purpose of satisfying the minds of those who may have heard the report, and of informing those who have put it in circulation, that it is earnestly requested they would desist therefrom.

In the notice, Joseph Smith Sr. also questioned the motives of rumormongers who intended to cause the family further pain, and the printed signature of "Joseph Smith" closed the notice.[181]

The death of his brother Alvin Smith was a pivotal event in the life of Joseph Smith. Nearly two decades after Alvin's passing, Joseph wrote of the nobility of his brother and the sorrow he felt over his death:

Joseph's tribute to Alvin, written so long after Alvin's death, shows that his brother's passing remained an open wound all the way to the end of Joseph's life.

However, the lonely grave of Alvin Smith was not the last time that Joseph Smith saw his noble older brother. On January 21, 1836, in the temple at Kirtland, Ohio, Joseph saw a vision of Alvin. This vision is now found in Doctrine and Covenants 137 and reads, in part,

> The heavens were opened upon us, and I beheld the celestial kingdom of God, and the glory thereof, whether in the body or out I cannot tell. I saw the transcendent beauty of the gate, through which the heirs of that kingdom will enter, which was like unto circling flames of fire. Also the blazing throne of God, wherein was seated the Father and the Son. I saw the beautiful streets of that kingdom, which had the appearance of being paved with Gold. I saw Father Adam, and Abraham, and Michael, and my Father and Mother, my brother Alvin [Smith] that has

181 Richard Lloyd Anderson, "The Alvin Smith Story: Fact and Fiction," *Ensign*, August 1987.

> long since slept and marveled how it was, that he had obtained an inheritance in that kingdom, seeing that he had departed this life before the Lord had set his hand to gather Israel the second time, and had not been baptized for the remission of sins.[182]

The truths revealed to Joseph Smith through his visions provide solace to all who have lost someone they loved. God, knowing all things, considers our knowledge and the state of our hearts before the Judgment. This system allows for perfect mercy and perfect justice for all people. The means for deceased individuals to make sacred covenants, such as baptism, were revealed to Joseph years later. But in 1836, all Joseph needed to know was that the door of salvation was still open for his brother. The Latter-day Saint view of the Savior's conquest over death, a vital part of the message of the Restoration, took another step forward when Joseph saw his brother in the celestial kingdom. This brief glimpse allows all to understand the mercy of God and His infinite goodness. No person is lost. God will judge us based on the desires of our hearts.

Joseph Smith saw a vision of Alvin in the Celestial Kingdom in 1837. Photo by Casey Paul Griffiths.

182 History, 1838–1856, volume B-1 [1 September 1834–2 November 1838], 695, The Joseph Smith Papers; see Doctrine and Covenants 137:1–6.

The vision of the celestial kingdom found in Doctrine and Covenants 137 came before God revealed to Joseph Smith that the sealing power makes it possible for living individuals to be baptized on behalf of those who are deceased. A few months after the vision in Doctrine and Covenants 137, Elijah appeared to Joseph in the Kirtland temple and gave him "the keys of this dispensation" necessary to perform these ordinances. Joseph later explained that Elijah "restored the authority to join families together forever in eternal relationships that transcend death."[183] It still took several more years until the principles surrounding work for the dead were fully revealed to Joseph. Once ordinances for the deceased were revealed, Alvin Smith received the ordinances by proxy, including baptism, confirmation, initiatory, and the endowment. Alvin was also sealed to his mother and father, explaining their presence together in the celestial kingdom in Joseph's vision (Doctrine and Covenants 137:5).[184]

Mini-Devotional—Hope for the Ones We Have Lost

Anytime a loved one passes prematurely, it can be difficult for those who mourn. The Smith family was devastated to lose their beloved oldest son or brother, Alvin Smith. But the death of Alvin opened the door to new revelations about life after death. Take a moment to read the excerpts from Doctrine and Covenants 137 found in this chapter. Then take moment to discuss the following questions:

- How do the revelations given to Joseph Smith help us have hope for the people we have lost?
- How can we play an active role in making sure our loved ones can join us in the celestial kingdom?

Share your testimony that the people we have lost can be reached through the truths and ordinances of the gospel. If you have had a special

183 "The Restoration of the Fulness of the Gospel of Jesus Christ: A Bicentennial Proclamation to the World," The Church of Jesus Christ of Latter-day Saints.

184 According to FamilySearch.org, Alvin Smith received his baptism, confirmation, initiatory, and endowment on April 10–11, 1877, in the St. George Utah Temple. He was sealed to his parents in the Salt Lake Temple on August 25, 1897. "Alvin Smith," accessed July 14, 2021, https://www.FamilySearch.org/tree/person/ordinances/KWVC-7KB.

experience overcoming the grief from the death of a loved one, take a moment to share it or write it down.

The Martin Harris Farm

The Lake Stone House at the Martin Harris farm. Photo by Casey Paul Griffiths.

Near the cemetery where Alvin Smith's grave is found is the Martin Harris farm. The home located on the Martin Harris farm property is not the original house Martin Harris lived in but was built in the nineteenth century, after Martin moved away from the farm. Today the home is a private residence and does not offer tours. There are picnic tables and pavilions nearby for visitors who want to stop in and spend some time on the farm.

Martin Harris was one of the most influential figures in the coming forth of the Book of Mormon. Martin's family were among the first settlers in the Palmyra area. His father, Nathan Harris, moved the family to the area in 1792 and began laboring to carve a prosperous farm out of the wilderness. In 1813, when he was thirty years old, Martin was given 320 acres of his father's farm. In the years that followed, Martin became a successful farmer in his own right and was active in community affairs.

In 1827, Martin Harris hired Joseph Smith Sr. and his sons to work on the farm. Joseph Smith worked with fields with Martin for $0.50 a day, while Father Smith and Hyrum Smith dug a well on the property. It was during this time that Joseph Smith shared his visions and experiences with Martin. Martin was soon convinced of Joseph's prophetic calling and became a fervent supporter of Joseph's work. He served as one of the earliest scribes of the Book of Mormon and in large measure paid for the printing of the Book of Mormon. Several revelations in the Doctrine and Covenants address Martin directly, including sections 3, 5, 10, 17, 19, 52, 58, 70, 82, and 104.

It is somewhat unfortunate that today most people familiar with the history of the Church associate Martin Harris only with the loss of the earliest manuscript of 116 pages of the Book of Mormon. When persecution in Palmyra made it necessary for Joseph Smith to relocate to his wife's family home in Harmony, Pennsylvania, Martin helped pay for the move and then spent a considerable amount of time in Harmony during the winter of 1827–28 assisting Joseph as scribe in the translation of the Book of Mormon. Martin arrived in Harmony in February 1828 and began working on the translation with the Prophet. By June, they had produced a substantial manuscript of what Joseph Smith described as "one hundred and sixteen pages, the which I took from the Book of Lehi, which was an account abridged from the plates of Lehi, by the hand of Mormon."[185]

Martin Harris's spending the winter away from his family appears to have caused tension between Martin and his wife, Lucy Harris, who remained in Palmyra. According to Joseph Smith's 1832 history, Martin asked for permission to take the manuscript with him to Palmyra because "he desired to carry them to read to his friends that peradventure he might convince them of the truth."[186] Joseph inquired of the Lord and was told "no" twice, but upon his third request, the Lord told Joseph to "let him go with them only he shall covenant with me that he will not shew them to only but four persons."[187] The 1838 history written by the Prophet identifies five people to whom Martin was allowed to show the manuscript: Martin's brother Preserved Harris; Martin's wife, Lucy Harris; Martin's father, Nathan Harris; Martin's mother, Rhoda Lapham Harris; and Martin's

185 *Book of Mormon* (Palmyra, NY: E.B. Grandin Press, 1830), iii, Joseph Smith Papers.

186 Joseph Smith History, circa Summer 1832, 5–6, JSP.

187 Joseph Smith History, circa Summer 1832, 5–6, JSP.

sister-in-law, Polly Harris Cobb. Martin willingly entered into this covenant with the Lord.[188]

Photo of Martin Harris. Courtesy Church History Library.

Very little is known about Lucy Harris except what Lucy Mack Smith, Joseph Smith's mother, recorded in her 1845 history. Lucy Mack Smith said Lucy Harris was initially convinced of the importance of Joseph's work because of a vision Lucy Harris received. Lucy Harris first assisted in the work, but later her faith wavered, and she began to pester her husband and Joseph for proof of the plates and the translation. Lucy Mack Smith even recalled a confrontation where Lucy Harris traveled all the way to Joseph and Emma Smith's home in Harmony and frantically searched it in an attempt to locate the plates. Unable to find the record, Lucy left in a rage and "went from place to place and from house to house, telling her grievances to everyone she met but particularly bewailing the deception which Joseph Smith was practicing a deception upon the people which was about to strip her of all that she possessed."[189] When Martin Harris took the manuscript with him to Palmyra, a large part of his motive was his desire to prove to his wife and to the community that he was not being defrauded.

While Martin Harris took the manuscript back to Palmyra, Joseph Smith remained in Harmony with Emma Smith, who was about to give birth to their first child. The child, named in honor of Joseph's deceased brother, Alvin Smith, lived for only a few hours. The birth was difficult for Emma, who nearly died during the delivery. For two weeks, Joseph remained at Emma's side, taking care of her. All the while, his anxiety over the manuscript grew steadily because no word arrived from Martin. Finally,

188 Joseph Smith History, 1838–1856, vol. A-1, 9, JSP.

189 Lucy Mack Smith, History, 1845, 125–26, JSP.

at Emma's urging, Joseph left Emma in the care of her parents and journeyed to Palmyra to find out what had happened to the manuscript.[190]

When Joseph Smith arrived in Palmyra, one of his brothers was immediately sent to find Martin Harris, who sent back assurances that he would come to the Smith farm the following morning. Arriving four hours later than expected, he vacillated at the gate to the the Smith home, even after they welcomed him in and offered a meal. Martin sat in silence until he burst out, "I have lost my soul!" Lucy Mack Smith wrote, "Joseph who had smothered his fears till now sprang from the table exclaiming Oh! Martin have you lost that manuscript! have you broken your oath and brought down condemnation upon my head as well as your own." "Yes," replied Martin, "it is gone and I know not where." "Oh! My God My God," said Joseph clenching his hands together, "All is lost what shall I do I have sinned it is me that tempted the wrath of God." After Martin departed, Joseph wept and paced the floor for hours while "sobs and groans and the most bitter lamentations filled the house."[191]

When all attempts to locate the manuscript failed, Joseph Smith left Palmyra and returned to Harmony in defeat. He later wrote, "Immediately after my return home I was walking out a little distance, when Behold the former heavenly messenger appeared and handed to me the Urim and Thummim again (for it had been taken from me in consequence of my having wearied the Lord in asking for the privilege of letting Martin Harris take the writings which he lost by transgression) and I enquired of the Lord."[192] The revelation Joseph received upon this inquiry is now recorded in Doctrine and Covenants 3. It was given through the Urim and Thummim and is the earliest revelation given to Joseph of which we have record.

The revelation calls Martin Harris a "wicked man," (Doctrine and Covenants 3:12). Martin disregarded the covenant he made to safeguard the manuscript and show it only to the designated people. Apparently Martin abided the conditions of the covenant at first but then cast it aside when an additional friend arrived and asked to see the manuscript. After showing the manuscript to one additional person, Martin showed little regard for his promise and began displaying the manuscript to others. All the

190 Lucy Mack Smith, History, 1844–1845, bk 7, 2, JSP.

191 History, 1844–1845, bk 7, 6, JSP.

192 Joseph Smith History, vol. A-1, 10, JSP.

attention caused the already strained situation with Lucy Harris to further deteriorate. She was enraged when Martin broke the lock on the cabinet in which he had been storing the manuscript. "Her irascible temper knew no bounds and an intolerable storm ensued throughout the house when descended with greatest force upon the head of the devoted husband," Lucy Mack Smith later wrote.[193]

One staunch defender of the legacy of Martin Harris is Dallin Harris Oaks, a descendant of Martin's brother Emer Harris. President Oaks taught, "Having a special interest in Martin Harris, I have been saddened at how he is remembered by most Church members. He deserves better than to be remembered solely as the man who unrighteously obtained and then lost the initial manuscript pages of the Book of Mormon."[194] Although Martin committed some grave mistakes in his handling of the manuscript, the Lord continued to tenderly help Martin through the repentance process (see Doctrine and Covenants 19). Martin was restricted from the privilege of serving as a scribe but remained a constant source of funding and support. Near the end of the translation process, Martin was called to serve as one of three witnesses of the Book of Mormon (see Doctrine and Covenants 17). He also assisted in identifying the members of the original Quorum of the Twelve in this dispensation. Finally, though Martin was still subject to many other mistakes and difficulties, he never wavered in his testimony of the Book of Mormon.

The sobering statements about Martin Harris in this Doctrine and Covenants 3 must be considered alongside the Lord's words to Martin in Doctrine and Covenants 5. The Lord chastised Martin for acting out of impure motives and even went so far as to say that Martin "sought to destroy" Joseph Smith's gift to translate (Doctrine and Covenants 10:6). These desires may not have been obvious even to Martin himself. The Lord counselled Martin to humble himself (see Doctrine and Covenants 5:28, 32), suggesting that part of Martin's failings sprang from jealousy over Joseph's gift to translate. Joseph and Martin sinned in treating lightly sacred things—first for failing to ensure the manuscript's safety, and second for not taking seriously the Lord's twice-repeated counsel not to share the manuscript with others.

---

193 Lucy Mack Smith History, 1844–1845, bk 7, 8, JSP.

194 Dallin H. Oaks, "The Witness: Martin Harris," *Ensign*, May 1999.

Detail of the stonework of the Lake Stone House at the Martin Harris Farm. Photo by Kenneth Mays.

When the Book of Mormon was finally published in 1830, Joseph Smith directly addressed the conspiracy to steal the manuscript and discredit the book. Joseph wrote about the "many unlawful measures taken by evil designing persons to destroy me, and also the work." He then described the plan of his enemies as follows: "Satan had put it into their hearts to tempt the Lord their God, by altering the words, that they did read contrary from that which I translated and caused to be written; and if I should bring forth the same words again, or, in other words, if I should translate the same over again, they would publish that which they had stolen, and Satan would stir up the hearts of this generation, that they might not receive this work."[195]

What was lost when thieves stole the manuscript? We know very little about what was written on those pages. Joseph gave this description of the contents of the lost manuscript: "I translated, by the gift and power of God, and caused to be written, one hundred and sixteen pages, the which I took from the Book of Lehi, which was an account abridged from the plates of Lehi, by the hand of Mormon."[196] This description would indicate that the lost manuscript was Mormon's abridgment of the early history of his civilization and would likely reflect the style of writing found in the book of Mosiah to 4 Nephi, with an omnipresent narrator arranging the history to encapsulate valuable lessons that often end with "and thus we see."

The thieves who stole the manuscript apparently expected Joseph Smith to retranslate that portion of the record and apparently intended to publish the manuscript with alterations and then claim Joseph Smith stole it and had no gift to translate. Instead of having Joseph retranslate that portion of

---

195 *Book of Mormon*, 1830, iii, JSP.
196 *Book of Mormon*, 1830, iii, JSP.

the record, the Lord had prepared an alternate plan. A smaller record was kept by the prophet Nephi and other record keepers (1 Nephi 6:1–6). These record on these smaller plates was written to "persuade men to come unto the God of Abraham, and the God of Isaac, and the God of Jacob, and be saved" (1 Nephi 6:4). Later, the prophet Mormon was commanded to include this record along with the abridged history he wrote of the Lehite civilization (Words of Mormon 1:3–8).

Joseph Smith later translated this smaller record to replace the material from the lost manuscript. Today this record constitutes 1 Nephi through Omni in the Book of Mormon. These writings contain some of the most profound and beautiful teachings about the mission of Jesus Christ found anywhere in scripture. Without the loss of the original manuscript, such teachings as "Adam fell that men might be, and men are that they might have joy" (2 Nephi 2:25) might not be part of our scriptures. Nephi's simple testimony, "I glory in plainness, I glory in truth, I glory in my Jesus, for he hath redeemed my soul from hell" (2 Nephi 33:6), is in our hands because of the Lord's plan to repair the damage from Martin Harris's and Joseph's mistakes.

Mini-Devotional—"The Works of God Cannot Be Frustrated"

Because of Martin Harris's disobedience, the work of translation was dealt a serious setback. When the manuscript was lost, Joseph Smith and Martin both felt the serious anguish many of us experience when we make a mistake. But the revelations given during this time show the Lord had a backup plan in place.

- Have you ever experienced a serious setback or made a mistake that caused you to feel anguish?
- What did you learn from those setbacks and mistakes?

The Lord turned the mistakes made by Joseph and Martin into teaching opportunities. The Lord also helped them through the repentance process. Not only did the Savior make up for what was lost, but His backup plan provided some of the most powerful testimonies of the Savior ever written.

- How has the Savior provided help when you have repented?

Martin Harris Affirms His Testimony in Court

Martin Harris's actions after the manuscript was lost demonstrate the sincerity of his testimony of the work. Doctrine and Covenants 5 serves as a counterpart to the lost manuscript saga. Doctrine and Covenants 3, 5, and 10 all contain the Lord's counsel concerning the lost manuscript. Joseph Smith received Doctrine and Covenants 5 in March 1829 when Martin, seeking assistance and counsel, traveled from Palmyra to Joseph and Emma Smith's home in Harmony. Joseph and Martin had not met together since the previous summer when Joseph traveled to Palmyra only to discover that the manuscript Martin had taken was already lost. The revelation in Doctrine and Covenants 5 served to renew their friendship and to bolster Martin's faith in Joseph's work of the Restoration.

Martin Harris came to Harmony to visit Joseph Smith partly because of a sharp increase in opposition against the work in Palmyra, including a lawsuit. One of the most vehement leaders of the opposition was Martin's wife, Lucy Harris. Lucy Mack Smith recalled, "She [Lucy Harris] mounted her horse [and] flew through the neighborhood like a dark spirit, from house to house making diligent enquiry at every house for miles where she had the least hope of gleaning anything that would subserve her purpose, which was to prove that Joseph had not the record which he pretended to have."[197] When Doctrine and Covenants 5 was first published in 1833, the section heading read, "Martin desired of the Lord to know whether Joseph had, in his possession, the record of the Nephites."[198]

In Doctrine and Covenants 5, the Lord affirmed the truth of the work to Joseph Smith and Martin Harris. He also commanded Martin concerning the plates that "he shall say: I have seen them, and they have been shown unto me by the power of God" (Doctrine and Covenants 5:26). This revelation had an uplifting effect on both Joseph and Martin. Immediately following its reception, Joseph appears to have overcome a brief crisis of confidence he suffered in the aftermath of the episode with the lost manuscript. With the help of Oliver Cowdery and others, Joseph commenced translation again, translating the entire Book of Mormon as we know it in the span of just a few months. The Lord's words of affirmation in the

197 Lucy Mack Smith History, 1844–1845, bk 8, 5, JSP.

198 *Book of Commandments*, 1833, 10, JSP.

revelation encouraged Joseph to stop hesitating and again dive fully into the translation.

The Lord's words in this revelation strengthened Martin Harris's witness of the work. Martin obeyed the Lord's command and shared his witness with the people around him. When Martin returned to Palmyra, he was called to testify in a trial due to Lucy Harris's lawsuit, which accused Joseph Smith of defrauding her husband. Martin "testified with boldness and energy," Lucy Mack Smith recorded. "When he rose he raised his hand to Heaven and said I can swear that Joseph Smith never got one dollar from me since God made me." Martin also told the accusers (including his own wife) that if they continued "to resist the truth it one day be the means of damning your souls." This testimony brought a swift end to the trial.[199]

Mini-Devotional—"Be Firm in Keeping the Commandments"

Martin Harris was met by opposition to the truth even by the closest members of his own family. He must have felt guilty about his role in the loss of the 116 pages of the Book of Mormon manuscript. It was also challenging to testify in front of the people of his community who thought he was being deceived. But the Lord commanded him to testify, and Martin obeyed the command.

- Have you ever faced opposition because of your testimony of the gospel?
- How can you follow Martin's example in bearing your witness of the truth?

Share an experience about a time you had the opportunity bear witness of the gospel to the people around you. It can be a testimony you shared in words or actions.

199 Lucy Mack Smith History, 1844–1845, bk. 8, 7, JSP.

Significant events at this location:

- Joseph Smith and Martin Harris negotiated with Egbert B. Grandin at this location to print the first copies of the Book of Mormon (see Doctrine and Covenants 19).
- The first copies of the Book of Mormon were printed and bound at this location.
- Thomas B. Marsh, the future president of the Quorum of the Twelve, obtained the first sixteen pages of the Book of Mormon at this location before it was printed (see Doctrine and Covenants 31).
- Joseph Smith, Hyrum Smith, and Oliver Cowdery confronted Abner Cole about stealing the text of the Book of Mormon before it was published.
- Joseph Smith and Oliver Cowdery purchased the Bible primarily used in the Joseph Smith Translation at the E. B. Grandin building.

THE PRINTING OF THE BOOK OF MORMON

E. B. Grandin Building: Book of Mormon Publication Site

The Book of Mormon Historic Publication Site on Main Street in Palmyra. Photo by Casey Paul Griffiths.

E. B. Grandin building, located on Main Street in Palmyra, is the place where the first copies of the Book of Mormon were printed. Joseph Smith and his close friends made many visits to the Grandin building from the summer of 1829 to the winter of 1830, when the first copies of the Book of Mormon were bound and made available. The process of printing the Book of Mormon had nearly as many dramatic twists as the translation of the Book of Mormon. The Grandin building was acquired by the Church in 1979 and has since been renovated and turned into a lovely visitor's center.[200] The presentations here are a great way for visitors to understand the translation process; the printing and publication of the Book of Mormon; and all the miracles, great and small, that took place during this crucial time.

200 See "Historic Discoveries at the Grandin Building," *Ensign*, July 1980.

Finding a Printer for the Book of Mormon

E. B. Grandin's printing establishment was only a short distance from the Smith farm and the Hill Cumorah. Because of his close proximity, Grandin was the first printer that Joseph Smith and his friends approached about publishing the Book of Mormon. When Egbert was first approached in the June of 1829, he staunchly refused to publish the book, believing Joseph was a false prophet and the book was a deception. According to Pomeroy Tucker, Egbert's brother-in-law, the printer was also concerned that Martin Harris was being deceived into sacrificing his life's savings for a foolhardy scheme.[201]

Following his rejection from E. B. Grandin, Joseph Smith approached several other printers in the greater Rochester area, including Jonathan A. Hadley, Thurlow Weed, and Elihu Marshall. He was met with varying degrees of skepticism by each of these men and worked to win their confidence that he was not a deceiver and that he could pay for the printing. Thurlow recalled later in his life that Joseph even demonstrated the translation process by using what Thurlow called a "tablet," which Joseph placed into a hat, upon which Joseph read a chapter of the Book of Mormon.[202] Elihu eventually agreed to print the Book of Mormon, but he was located miles away from Palmyra. Joseph, perhaps still cautious because of the incident with the lost manuscript pages of the Book of Mormon, wanted to be close by during the printing process. Perhaps hoping to use Elihu's agreement to leverage cooperation from Grandin, Joseph and his friends returned to Palmyra.

E. B. Grandin's Terms, Martin Harris, and Doctrine and Covenants 19

Approached a second time, Egbert B Grandin again hesitated, but he finally agreed to enter into a contract to carry out the printing of the Book

201 Michael Hubbard MacKay and Gerrit J. Dirkmaat, *From Darkness unto Light: Joseph Smith's Translation and Publication of the Book of Mormon* (Salt Lake City: Deseret Book, 2015), 165–66.

202 MacKay and Dirkmaat, *From Darkness unto Light*, 171.

of Mormon, provided that he could dictate the terms of the agreement. Egbert's terms were not generous. He demanded payment up front before even beginning the printing, in contrast to the more common practice of sharing the profits from the book's sales to help cover the cost. He insisted on $3,000 to produce five thousand copies of the book. Several scholars have pointed out that for a book similar to the Book of Mormon, most printers of the time sought about a 12 percent profit margin. In contrast, Egbert's terms would have allowed for a profit margin of more than 33 percent![203] Egbert's terms throw cold water on the perception that he was trying to protect Martin Harris from deception.

Egbert B. Grandin's demands placed extreme pressure on the already fragile marriage of Martin and Lucy Harris. To begin the printing, Martin would have to give up nearly all of the property he owned. Not knowing whether he would ever be able to recoup the investment, Martin experienced an intense trial of faith. It is likely under these circumstances that he petitioned Joseph Smith to inquire of the Lord, and the revelation eventually placed in the Doctrine and Covenants as section 19 was received on Martin's behalf.

We do not know the exact date that Doctrine and Covenants 19 was given. Historians from the Joseph Smith Papers project have dated the revelation to the summer of 1829, though it is possible it came a few months later, in early 1830.[204] In the revelation, Martin Harris was counseled to repent of his sins. The Savior spoke of His suffering when He atoned for the sins of all men and women. "For behold, I, God, have suffered these things for all, that they might not suffer if they would repent; But if they would not repent they must suffer even as I; Which suffering caused myself, even God, the greatest of all, to tremble because of pain, and to bleed at every pore, and to suffer both body and spirit—and would that I might not drink the bitter cup, and shrink—Nevertheless, glory be to the Father, and I partook and finished my preparations unto the children of men. Wherefore, I command you again to repent" (Doctrine and Covenants 19:17–20).

In January 1830, Joseph Smith entered into an agreement with Martin Harris to give him "equal privilege" to sell copies of the Book of Mormon

---

203 MacKay and Dirkmaat, *From Darkness unto Light*, 175.

204 See, "Historical Introduction," in *Documents, Volume 1: July 1828–June 1831*, ed. Michael Hubbard MacKay, Gerrit J. Dirkmaat, Grant Underwood, Robert J. Woodford, and William G. Hartley, vol. 1 of the Documents series of *The Joseph Smith Papers* (Salt Lake City: Intellectual Reserve, 2013), 85.

to assist with the cost of printing. However, the books did not sell well initially, and Martin became nervous that he might not be able to recoup the cost of his investment. According to Joseph Knight Sr., Martin, wracked with anxiety, approached Joseph Smith, saying, "The books will not sell for nobody wants them." Joseph replied, "I think they will sell well." Martin insisted on receiving a revelation from the Lord, to which Joseph responded, "Fulfill what you have got," apparently a reference to Doctrine and Covenants 19.[205]

That night, Martin Harris stayed at the Smith home, sleeping in a bed on the floor next to Joseph Knight Sr. In the middle of the night, Martin woke up Father Knight, asking whether he felt something on the bed. Having felt nothing, Father Knight asked Martin why he was alarmed. Martin replied that he had felt something like a large dog jumping onto his chest. Father Knight neither felt nor saw anything. Disturbed by the dream, Martin insisted again the next morning that Joseph Smith receive a revelation on his behalf..[206]

Joseph Smith did not provide a further commandment for Martin Harris, instead urging him again to read and ponder Doctrine and Covenants 19. In spite of this, Martin complied with the earlier revelation and sold the property necessary to pay off the debt. In obeying the Lord's commandments, Martin became one of the most important financial contributors to the coming forth of the Book of Mormon.[207] Martin was also able to eventually recover the debt associated with the cost of the printing. According to one source, when asked years later whether he ever lost any of the $3,000, Martin said, "I never lost one cent. Mr. Smith paid me all that I advanced, and more too."[208]

Martin Harris soon put into practice the Savior's counsel to revile "not against revilers" (Doctrine and Covenants 19:30). He became an enthusiastic proponent of the Book of Mormon, inviting his friends and neighbors in Palmyra to purchase copies of the book. One early source from this time records,

---

205 Dean Jessee, "Joseph Knight's Recollection of Early Mormon History," *BYU Studies* 17, no. 1 (Autumn 1976): 10–11.

206 Jessee, "Joseph Knight's Recollection of Early Mormon History," 10–11.

207 "The Contributions of Martin Harris," in *Revelations in Context* (2016).

208 "Testimonies of Oliver Cowdery and Martin Harris," in *Millennial Star* (1859), 21: 545.

> Harris was proverbially a peaceful as well as an honest man. He was slow to retaliate an offence. . . . Urging the sale of the book with pertinacious confidence in the genuineness of the Smith revelation, he fell into debate about its character with a neighbor of irascible temperament. His opponent became angry, and struck him a severe blow upon the right side of his face. Instantly turning toward the assailant the other cheek, [Martin] quoted the Christian maxim, reading it from the book in his hand [The Book of Mormon] page 481 (as it also appears in Matthew): "Whosoever shall smite thee on the right cheek, turn to him the other also."[209]

Mini-Devotional—The Savior Knows My Trials

Finding a printer for the Book of Mormon was no small task. Joseph Smith and his friends met with opposition, derision, and hostility because of their belief in God's work. When Egbert B. Grandin finally agreed to print the book, his price demanded a great sacrifice from Martin Harris. When Martin was troubled with what this sacrifice might cost, the Lord spoke to Martin personally, urging him to repent and encouraging him to pay his debt to the printer.

Read the Savior's words to Martin Harris in Doctrine and Covenants 19:15–20.

- How does the Savior's atonement qualify Him to assist us in our challenges?
- How can keeping the Lord's commandments and repenting keep us from greater suffering?

Share your testimony that just like the Savior knew the challenges Martin faced, He also knows the challenges we face and will help us if we trust in Him and work to repent of our sins.

---

209 Pomeroy Tucker, *Origin, Rise and Progress of Mormonism* (1867), 61. Portions of this material were previously published on Doctrine and Covenants Central. See "Doctrine & Covenants 19," Doctrine and Covenants Central, accessed February 8, 2022, https://doctrineandcovenantscentral.org/section-19/.

Oliver Cowdery, Hyrum Smith and the Printing of the Book of Mormon

Tools for demonstrating the publication process of the first copies of the Book of Mormon. Photo by Casey Paul Griffiths.

While the Book of Mormon was being printed, Joseph Smith made frequent visits to Palmyra, but his primary residence was in Harmony, Pennsylvania, over 150 miles away. During this time, Hyrum Smith and Oliver Cowdery, who both lived near Palmyra, helped oversee and monitor the printing process. Shortly after the translation was finished, Oliver was tasked with preparing a copy of the manuscript. Still wary after the incident with Martin Harris and the lost manuscript, Joseph felt it would be wise to give the printer a copy of the manuscript instead of the original manuscript. Oliver, Hyrum, and an unknown scribe labored over several months to create the printer's manuscript of the Book of Mormon. Analysis of the manuscript shows that Oliver wrote about 84 percent, while the unknown scribe copied about 15 percent, and Hyrum wrote less than 1 percent.[210] Joseph gave strict instructions to Oliver to "never take both manuscripts to

210 "Historical Introduction," Printer's Manuscript of the Book of Mormon, circa August 1829–circa January 1830, i, JSP.

the [printing] office." Oliver was also instructed to take someone with him whenever transporting the manuscript "for the purpose of protecting him in case of danger." Joseph warned that "if this precaution was not taken his enemies would be likely to waylay him in order to get the manuscript away from him."[211]

E. B. Grandin started the work of printing in late August 1829. All throughout the fall of that year, Oliver Cowdery, Hyrum Smith, and the unknown scribe continued their work of copying the original manuscript of the Book of Mormon to create a manuscript for use by the printer. A letter from Oliver written on November 6, 1829, indicates that he had copied roughly half of the manuscript and was working through the book of Alma.[212] The original manuscript of the Book of Mormon has virtually no punctuation, and the printer's manuscript added almost no punctuation as well. Oliver and Hyrum worked with John Gilbert, the typesetter at the Grandin Press, to add punctuation to the manuscript. John even convinced Hyrum to allow him to take portions of the manuscript home overnight so that he could add punctuation before printing the next day. While adding punctuation, Oliver, Hyrum, and others worked to preserve the language found in the inspired translation. John remembered pointing out a grammatical error in the manuscript to Martin Harris and Hyrum. He said Hyrum told him, "The Old Testament is ungrammatical, set it as it is written."[213]

John Gilbert set the type for around 500 of the 589 pages in the original printing of the Book of Mormon. Oliver Cowdery also set the type for a few pages and acted as a proofreader during the printing. After each printed sheet was completed, it was checked against the manuscript to make sure that it was accurate. Work on the printing was carried on for three days every week, with the other two days devoted to an already existing contract to print the *Wayne Sentinel*, a local newspaper.[214] Printing continued at a

211 Lucy Mack Smith, History, 1844–1845, bk. 9, [2], JSP.

212 "Historical Introduction," Printer's Manuscript of the Book of Mormon, circa August 1829–circa January 1830, 6n.

213 John H. Gilbert, Memorandum, September 8, 1892, photocopy, Church History Library, Salt Lake City; see also "Mormon Leaders at Their Mecca," *New York Herald*, June 25, 1893, 12. "Historical Introduction," Printer's Manuscript of the Book of Mormon, circa August 1829–circa January 1830, i.

214 "Historical Introduction," Printer's Manuscript of the Book of Mormon, circa August 1829–circa January 1830, i.

smooth pace until January 1830, when Abner Cole, owner of another local newspaper, tried to steal and print portions of the Book of Mormon.

Abner Cole's Attempts to Steal the Text of the Book of Mormon

Ink balls like these were used in the printing process of the Book of Mormon. Photo by Casey Paul Griffiths.

Around the same time that the printing of the Book of Mormon began, Abner Cole began publishing his newspaper, the *Reflector*. Abner printed his newspaper on nights and weekends, using the same press that was used during the week to print the Book of Mormon. Writing under the pseudonym "Obadiah Dogberry," Abner immediate began to deride the Book of Mormon. On September 2, 1829, he wrote in the *Reflector*, "The Golden Bible, by Joseph Smith Junior, author and proprietor, is now in press and will shortly appear. Priestcraft is short lived!"[215] Working in the same print shop, Abner had opportunity to view the earliest proof sheets of the Book of Mormon, which were hung up to dry in E. B. Grandin's shop. Abner began reading through these early pages and stealing phrases from the Book of Mormon to make satirical attacks before the book even rolled off the press.

215 MacKay and Dirkmaat, *From Darkness unto Light*, 206.

He even found humor in the numerous uses of the phrase "and it came to pass" found in the early chapters of the Book of Mormon.[216]

Abner Cole continued his efforts to satirize the Book of Mormon, publishing a mixture of plagiarism, hearsay, and outright prejudicial comments. On October 7, 1829, Abner proclaimed that "the building of the TEMPLE OF NEPHI is to be commenced about the beginning of the first year of the Millennium. Thousands are flocking to the standard of Joseph the Prophet. The Book of Mormon is expected to astonish the natives!"[217] On December 9, 1829, Abner even wrote that he would begin publishing actual excerpts from the Book of Mormon, though he noted that the book would "not be ready for delivery for some months to come."[218] Despite their close proximity, Oliver Cowdery and Hyrum Smith were unaware of Abner's attacks on the Book of Mormon for several months. However, around January 1830, Hyrum experiencing and uneasy feeling that led him to believe something was going wrong at the printing office. He asked Oliver to accompany him to printing office, despite it being a Sunday evening. When they arrived at the office, they found Abner in the work of printing another issue of the *Reflector*.[219]

Hyrum Smith picked up one of the sheets that Abner Cole had printed and saw excerpts from the Book of Mormon. He immediately confronted Abner, saying, "What right have you to print the Book of Mormon in this way, do you not know that we have received a copy right?" Abner responded, "It is none of your business sir, I have hired the press and I will print what I please." Hyrum implored him further, "I forbid you from printing any more of that book in your paper for that is sacred and you must stop." Abner angrily replied, "I don't care a damn for you—that damned Gold bible is going into my paper." Hyrum and Oliver Cowdery continued to contend with Abner, but he refused to relent. In frustration they went home, finding in a few days that another issue of the *Reflector* was circulating through the town. [220]

216 MacKay and Dirkmaat, *From Darkness unto Light*, 208.
217 MacKay and Dirkmaat, *From Darkness unto Light*, 209.
218 MacKay and Dirkmaat, *From Darkness unto Light*, 210.
219 See also MacKay and Dirkmaat, *From Darkness unto Light*, 210–11. Lucy Mack Smith, History, 1844–1845, bk. 9, [9], JSP.
220 Lucy Mack Smith, History, 1844–1845, bk. 9, [9], spelling corrected and punctuation added.

Alarmed over Abner Cole's continued attempts to discredit the Book of Mormon, Oliver Cowdery and Hyrum Smith sent for Joseph Smith, who traveled from his home in Pennsylvania to resolve the matter. Joseph arrived in Palmyra on a cold, blustery Sunday. As soon as possible, he went to the Grandin building, where he found Abner hard at work on another issue of the *Reflector*. Joseph greeted Abner politely, saying, "How do you do, Mr. Cole, you seem hard at work." After examining one of the sheets Abner had printed, Joseph became more firm, saying, "Mr. Cole that book and the right of publishing it belongs to me, and I forbid you meddling [with] it." At this, Abner threw off his coat, rolled up his sleeves and came towards Joseph "in a great rage," yelling, "Do you want to fight sir? Do you want to fight? I will publish just as what I'm a mind to and now if you want to fight just come on." Joseph remained calm, saying, "Well now Mr. Cole you had better keep your coat for it's cold and I am not going to fight nor anything of that sort. But you have got to stop printing my book. Sir, I assure you for I know my rights and shall maintain them." Abner bawled out another threat, "If you think you are the best man, just take off your coat and try it." Joseph replied in a low, significant, tone, "Mr. Cole, there is [a] law—and you will find that out if you did not know it before. But I shall not fight you for that would do no good and there is another way of disposing of the affair that will answer my purpose better than fighting."[221]

With Joseph Smith refusing to match his opponent's antics, Abner Cole began to cool off and finally agreed to submit the matter to arbitration. Abner still published excerpts from the Book of Mormon in the next two issues of his paper but stopped after the January 21, 1830, issue of the *Reflector*. Lucy Mack Smith, whose history describes this episode, does not share how the matter was finally settled, but Abner's interference waned after his confrontation with Joseph.[222]

Mini-Devotional: Standing Up For Truth

Joseph Smith, Oliver Cowdery, and Hyrum Smith did not seek conflict with Abner Cole, but Abner's actions forced them to intervene. Joseph

221 Lucy Mack Smith, History, 1844–1845, bk. 9, [10], JSP.

222 Lucy Mack Smith, History, 1844–1845, bk. 9, [11], JSP, MacKay and Dirkmaat, *From Darkness unto Light*, 212.

refused to engage in violence to get Abner to stop his illegal actions, but he did insist that Abner cease violating their rights. When have you had conflict with others who were doing the wrong thing? Ponder for a moment the following questions:

- Why is it important for us to stand up for ourselves when someone is being unfair or taking advantage of us?
- What can you learn from the way Joseph Smith handled his conflict with Abner Cole?

Joseph resolved this conflict without stooping the to same level as Abner. He also treated a person who was being unfair to him with respect, kindness, and firmness. When we face conflicts in our own lives, seeking peaceful resolutions can help us be true disciples of Jesus Christ.

Purchasing the Bible Used for the Joseph Smith Translation

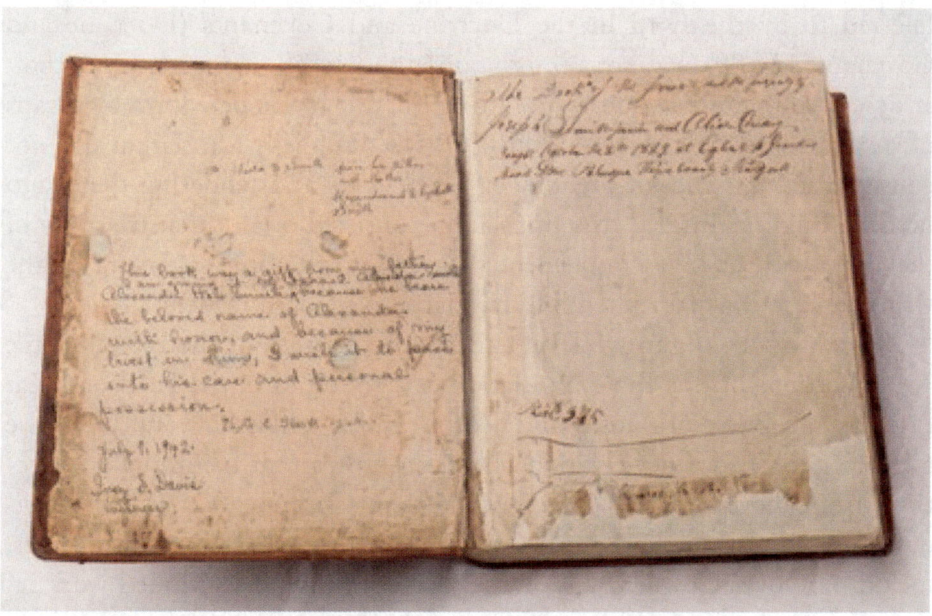

Joseph Smith and Oliver Cowdery purchased this Bible for $3.75 from E.B. Grandin to begin work on their new project to translate the Bible. Photo by Cordale Ottley, courtesy Community of Christ.

The Grandin building played a significant role not only in the coming forth of the Book of Mormon but also in Joseph Smith's next important translation project. Even while the Book of Mormon was being printed, Joseph and his associates began plans to complete a translation of the Bible, intended to correct many of the errors that had crept into the text and to restore many of the plain and precious truths lost. On October 8, 1829, Oliver Cowdery purchased a large King James Bible from the Grandin Press. This Bible, which is currently in the custody of Community of Christ, is one of the most important objects in understanding the nature of the Joseph Smith translation. The Bible is a large, pulpit-style edition containing the Old and New Testaments along with the Apocrypha. It is nine inches wide, eleven inches long, and about 2.5 inches thick and weighs just under five pounds. On the inside cover in the large handwriting of Joseph is the inscription, "The Book of the Jews and the property of Joseph Smith Junior and Oliver Cowdery, bought October 3, 1829 at Egbert B Grandin's Book Store, Palmyra, Wayne County, New York. Price $3.75. Holiness to the Lord."[223]

It is believed that this Bible served as the primary study text for Joseph Smith's New Translation of the Bible. The "New Translation," as it was referred to by the Lord in the Doctrine and Covenants (Doctrine and Covenants 124:89), was not a translation in the traditional sense. One scholar described the translation as "recasting the text into a new form by means of inspiration from the Holy Spirit."[224] The Prophet's translation did not consist of taking ancient Hebrew or Greek texts and rendering them into modern English. Instead, the translation consisted of an intensive study of the Bible with changes implemented to restore the original intent of the writers and to make it more understandable to modern readers.

Joseph Smith began work on this new translation of the Bible in June 1830. Portions of this Bible translation can be found in the Pearl of Great Price as the Book of Moses and Joseph Smith—Matthew. In 1979, the Church published a new edition of the scriptures that incorporated selections from the translation into footnotes and an appendix in the Latter-day Saint edition of the King James Bible. Working with various scribes, including Oliver Cowdery and Sidney Rigdon, Joseph continued work on the new translation, finishing a first draft by July 2, 1833.[225] The Prophet's study of the Bible is linked to several important revelations given to him

223 Bible Used for Bible Revision, JSP.

224 Kent Jackson, "Joseph Smith's New Translation of the Bible," in *Joseph Smith, the Prophet and Seer,* (Salt Lake City: Deseret Book, 2017), 51-76.

225 Old Testament Revision 2, 119, JSP.

and his scribes, including sections 29, 38, 42, 76, and 132 of the Doctrine and Covenants. One scholar has noted, "Doctrines such as the law of celestial marriage, the age of accountability at eight years, the degrees of glory, possibly the duties of the various quorums and councils of the priesthood, and much about the second coming of the Lord Jesus, were made known to Joseph Smith in the process of translation. The translation was a learning experience for the Prophet."[226]

Publication of the Book of Mormon

1830 Edition of the Book of Mormon. Photo by Cordale Ottley, courtesy of Brent Ashworth.

Even before the first copies of the Book of Mormon were complete, it began to have an impact on those who read its message. Thomas B. Marsh was from Charlestown, Massachusetts, and was affiliated with the Methodist Church when he first heard about the new scripture in 1829. According to his own recollection, "I thought the spirit required me to make a journey West." His journey eventually led him to the Palmyra area, where he first

226 Robert J. Matthews, "The Role of the Joseph Smith Translation in the Restoration," in *Plain and Precious Truths Restored: The Doctrinal and Historical Significance of the Joseph Smith Translation*, ed. Robert L. Millet and Robert J. Matthews (Salt Lake City: Deseret Book, 1995), 41–42.

heard of the printing of the Book of Mormon. While in Palmyra, he met with Martin Harris and saw proof sheets of the Book of Mormon. He also met with Oliver Cowdery, who "gave [him] all the information concerning the Book [he] wanted." He traveled back to his home with a proof sheet that contained the first sixteen pages of the Book of Mormon. After learning of the Church's organization, Thomas moved with his family to Palmyra in the fall of 1830. Shortly before the second conference of the Church, he was baptized by David Whitmer and ordained an elder by Oliver.[227] In 1835, Thomas was ordained a member of the original Quorum of the Twelve Apostles in this dispensation, serving as the first president of the Quorum.

Another early convert moved by the teachings of the Book of Mormon was Parley P. Pratt. During his travels through the region around Palmyra, he had heard tales "of a book, a STRANGE BOOK, a VERY STRANGE BOOK!" He recalled that when he was loaned a copy and read the book himself, "For the first time, my eyes beheld the 'BOOK OF MORMON' that book of books—that record which reveals the antiquities of the 'New World' back to the remotest ages, and which unfolds the destiny of its people and the world for all time to come; that Book which contains the fulness of the gospel of a crucified and risen Redeemer; that Book which reveals a lost remnant of Joseph, and which was the principal means, in the hands of God, of directing the entire course of my future life."[228]

Parley P. Pratt later wrote,

> I opened it with eagerness, and read its title page. I then read the testimony of several witnesses in relation to the manner of its being found and translated. After this I commenced its contents by course. I read all day; eating was a burden, I had no desire for food; sleep was a burden when the night came, for I preferred reading to sleep. As I read, the spirit of the Lord was upon me, and I knew and comprehended that the book was true, as plainly and manifestly as a man comprehends and knows that he exists. My joy was now full, as it were, and I rejoiced sufficiently to more than pay me for all the sorrows, sacrifices and toils of my life.[229]

---

227 "TB Marsh," Historian's Office, Histories of the Twelve, ca. 1858–1880, CHL. See "Historical Context and Background of D&C 31," Doctrine and Covenants Central, accessed February 15, 2022, https://doctrineandcovenantscentral.org/historical-context/dc-31/.

228 Parley P. Pratt, *Autobiography of Parley P. Pratt: Revised and Enhanced Edition* (Salt Lake City: Deseret Book, 2000), 30–31.

229 Pratt, *Autobiography of Parley P. Pratt*, 30–31.

During his lifetime, Parley was instrumental in helping convert a number of important figures, including Sidney Rigdon, Edward Partridge, and future Church President John Taylor. Parley was ordained a member of this dispensation's original Quorum of the Twelve Apostles in 1835.[230]

Some of these early converts faced immense opposition to their faith. Rachel Ridgeway Grant initially rejected the message of Restoration when it first was presented to her. However, she later remarked that reading the Book of Mormon changed her mind. After getting her own copy of the book, she remembered, "I read nearly all night in the Book of Mormon, and felt that it was true, and then I got the spirit of gathering." She gathered with the Saints, later becoming the mother of Church President Heber J. Grant.[231]

For the time, a print run of five thousand copies was unusually large. To compare, the first printing of Nathaniel Hawthorne's novel *The Scarlett Letter* was only 2,500 copies.[232] One history of the printing of the Book of Mormon records that "it took eleven hours a day, six days a week, excluding Sundays and holidays, for nine months" to print the five thousand copies of the first edition. At nearly six hundred pages per copy, that is nearly three million pages.[233] On March 19, 1830, a Palmyra newspaper ran an advertisement reading, "We are requested to announce that the 'Book of Mormon' will be ready for sale in the course of a week." With the first copies of the Book of Mormon now in the hands of a growing number of converts, the stage was set for the organization of the Church.[234]

Today, the original Grandin Press is on display in the Church History Museum in Salt Lake City. After the Church acquired the Grandin building in the 1970s, work began on an extensive restoration of the property. One of the project supervisors noted, "The building was fragile. Restoring it was like unscrambling an egg. All materials added to the building after 1830 had to be removed. It was a slow process of demolition, then

---

230 See "Commentary on Doctrine & Covenants 32," Doctrine and Covenants Central, accessed February 15, 2022, https://doctrineandcovenantscentral.org/sections/commentary-on-dc-32/?Verses-1-3.

231 MacKay and Dirkmaat, *From Darkness unto Light*, 216.

232 "The Grandin Press: A Vital Tool of the Restoration," The Church of Jesus Christ of Latter-day Saints, accessed February 15, 2022, https://history.churchofjesuschrist.org/content/museum/grandin-press?lang=eng.

233 "Historic Discoveries at the Grandin Building," *Ensign*, July 1980, 50.

234 "The Grandin Press: A Vital Tool of the Restoration."

restoration, more demolition, then restoration." The building was rededicated on March 26–27, 1998, by President Gordon B. Hinckley.[235]

Mini-Devotional—The Power of Reading the Book of Mormon

The Book of Mormon had a powerful effect on its early readers. People like Thomas B. Marsh, Parley P. Pratt, and Rachel Ridgeway Grant were deeply moved by its teachings. As the words of the book entered into their minds and hearts, they were converted to the gospel and sought out missionaries who helped them join the Church. The Book of Mormon remains a powerful tool to bring people to Christ. Take a few moments to reflect on the following questions:

- How have you gained your own testimony of the Book of Mormon?
- What teachings in the Book of Mormon have made a difference in your life?

Share the following quote from President Ezra Taft Benson:

> The Book of Mormon is the keystone of our religion. This was the Prophet Joseph Smith's statement. He testified that "the Book of Mormon was the most correct of any book on earth, and the keystone of our religion" (Introduction to the Book of Mormon). A keystone is the central stone in an arch. It holds all the other stones in place, and if removed, the arch crumbles.
>
> There are three ways in which the Book of Mormon is the keystone of our religion. It is the keystone in our witness of Christ. It is the keystone of our doctrine. It is the keystone of testimony.
>
> The Book of Mormon is the keystone in our witness of Jesus Christ, who is Himself the cornerstone of everything we do.[236]

---

235 Shaun D. Stahle, "Historic Grandin Building Restored," *Church News*, March 28, 1998, https://www.thechurchnews.com/archives/1998-03-28/historic-grandin-building-restored-127953.

236 Ezra Taft Benson, "The Book of Mormon is the Word of God," *Ensign*, October 1986.

Significant events at this location:

- Joseph Smith and Oliver Cowdery moved to the Peter Whitmer Sr. Farm in June 1829. While there, they completed the final part of the translation of the Book of Mormon.
- The Three Witnesses of the Book of Mormon—Oliver Cowdery, Martin Harris, and David Whitmer—saw the gold plates, several sacred relics, and the angel Moroni, and they heard the voice of God near the Whitmer Farm (see Doctrine and Covenants 17).
- Joseph Smith heard the "voice of God in the chamber of old Father Whitmer" directing the first ordinations to the Melchizedek Priesthood (Doctrine and Covenants 128:21).
- On April 6, 1830, the organization of the Church took place at the Peter Whitmer Sr. Farm (see Doctrine and Covenants 20–21).
- The Peter Whitmer Sr. Farm served as the first headquarters of the Church.
- Doctrine and Covenants 14–18, 20–21, 28–31, and 33–40 were received at or near the Peter Whitmer Sr. Farm.

THE PETER WHITMER SENIOR FARM

The rebuilt home of Peter and Mary Whitmer – the birthplace of the Church. Photo by Casey Paul Griffiths.

The Peter Whitmer Sr. Farm is near the present-day town of Waterloo in upstate New York and is nestled into the beautiful countryside in between Lake Seneca and Lake Cayuga. During the time the Whitmers lived in this area it was known as Fayette township. On the site stands a reconstruction of the Peter Whitmer Sr. family home and a beautiful chapel, which serves as a visitors' center. The reconstructed home and the chapel were both dedicated in 1980 as part of the celebrations surrounding the 150th anniversary of the founding of the Church. Peter and Mary Whitmer lived on the farm with their children Christian, Jacob, John, David, Catherine, Peter Jr., Nancy, and Elizabeth Ann Whitmer. The Whitmer family played a key role in the translation of the Book of Mormon and the organization of the Church. Many members of the Whitmer family served as witnesses of the Book of Mormon. Because of the centrality of the Whitmer family, the farm is considered the birthplace of the Church. In many ways, it also served as the first headquarters of the Church.

The Whitmer Family and the Coming Forth of the Book of Mormon

Photo of David Whitmer, circa 1855, courtesy Community of Christ Library.

Joseph Smith and Oliver Cowdery first came to the Whitmer Farm in June 1829, seeking a haven from persecution. Opposition to the work in the area around Harmony, Pennsylvania, had reached a new peak, so Joseph and Oliver sought a refuge to complete the translation of the Book of Mormon. Oliver reached out to his friend David Whitmer and asked if they could come to his family's farm to complete their sacred work. The Whitmer Farm is only about thirty miles away from the Hill Cumorah, and the entire region was alive with rumors about the retrieval of the plates. Lucy Mack Smith later recalled that Joseph was commanded "to write a letter to one David Whitmer this man Joseph had never seen but he was instructed to say [to] him that he must come with his team immediately in order to convey Joseph and Oliver back to his house which was 135 miles that they might remain with him there until the translation [was] completed . . . [because] an evil designing people were seeking to take away Joseph's life in order to prevent the work of God from going forth."[237]

237 Lucy Mack Smith, History, 1844–1845, bk. 8, [8], JSP.

Miracles began at the Whitmer Farm even before Joseph Smith and Oliver Cowdery arrived. Oliver's letter arrived when the Whitmer family was overwhelmed with the responsibilities of running the farm. David Whitmer later explained, "I did not know what to do, I was pressed with my work. I had some 20 acres to plow, so I concluded I would finish plowing then go. I got up one morning to go to work as usual, and on going to the field, found between five and seven acres of my ground had been plowed during the night. I didn't know who did it; but it was done just as I would have done it myself, and the plow was left standing in the furrow."[238]

Lucy Mack Smith recalled the same incident with slightly different details. According to Lucy, David Whitmer's work entailed sowing the field with plaster of Paris, which, during the time, was commonly used to reduce the acidity of soil. David determined to complete the chore and then depart to assist Joseph Smith and Oliver Cowdery. Lucy reported,

> The next morning David took a wooden measure under his arm and went out to sow the plaster; which he had left two days previous in heaps, near his sister's dwelling; but on approaching the place, where he had left it he discovered that it was gone. He then ran to his sister and inquired of her, if she knew what had become of it. She said with some surprise: "why do you ask me? was it not all sown yesterday?" "not to my knowledge," answered David, "I am astonished at that," continued his sister; "the children came to me in the forenoon and begged me to go out and see the men sow plaster in the field—that they never saw any body sow plaster so fast in their lives. I accordingly went; and I saw three men at work in the field as the children said; but supposing that you had hired some help on account of your hurry, I went immediately into the house, and paid no farther attention."[239]

Lucy added, "David made considerable inquiry among his relatives and neighbors in regard to the matter, but was not able to ascertain who had done it. However, the family were all convinced, that there was an exertion of supernatural power connected with this strange occurrence. David

238 Joseph F. Smith, diary, September 7–8, 1878, MS 1325, Church History Library, Salt Lake City.

239 Lucy Mack Smith, History, 1845, 149–51, JSP.

immediately set out for Pennsylvania, and arrived there in two days, without injuring his horses in the least; though the distance was 135 miles."[240]

David Whitmer assisted in moving Joseph Smith and Oliver Cowdery to his family's farm. David later recalled that, while riding with Joseph in a wagon on the trip back from Harmony,

> A very pleasant, nice-looking old man suddenly appeared by the side of our wagon and saluted us with, "Good morning, it is very warm," at the same time wiping his face or forehead with his hand. We returned the salutation, and, by a sign from Joseph, I invited him to ride if he was going our way. But he said very pleasantly, "No, I am going to Cumorah." This name was something new to me, I did not know what Cumorah meant. We all gazed at him and at each other, and as I looked around enquiringly of Joseph, the old man instantly disappeared. . . .
>
> . . . It was the messenger who had the plates, who had taken them from Joseph just prior to our starting from Harmony.[241]

The final phase of the Book of Mormon translation took place at the Whitmer Farm during June 1829. David Whitmer later described the translation process of the Book of Mormon, saying:

> Joseph Smith would put the seer stone into a hat, and put his face in the hat, drawing it closely around his face to exclude the light; and in the darkness the spiritual light would shine. A piece of something resembling parchment would appear, and on that appeared the writing. One character at a time would appear, and under it was the interpretation in English. Brother Joseph would read off the English to Oliver Cowdery, who was his principal scribe, and when it was written down and repeated to Brother Joseph to see if it was correct, then it would disappear, and another character with the interpretation would appear. Thus the Book of Mormon was translated by the gift and power of God, and not by any power of man."[242]

While David Whitmer had the closest relationship to Joseph Smith and Oliver Cowdery—eventually becoming one of the Three Witnesses of

240 Lucy Mack Smith, History, 1845, 149–51, JSP.

241 "Report of Elders Orson Pratt and Joseph F. Smith," *Deseret Evening News*, November 27, 1878, 2.

242 David Whitmer, *An Address to All Believers in Christ* (Richmond, MO, 1887), 12.

the Book of Mormon—nearly every member of the Whitmer family left an account of the work of translation. Elizabeth Ann Whitmer, who later married Oliver Cowdery, recalled: "I cheerfully certify that I was familiar with the manner of Joseph Smith's translating the Book of Mormon. He translated most of it at my Father's house. And I often sat by and saw and heard them translate and write for hours together. Joseph never had a curtain drawn between him and his scribe while he was translating. He would place the director in his hat, and then place his face in the hat, so as to exclude the light, and then [read the words] as they appeared before him."[243]

Spiritual Manifestations in the Whitmer Home

Upstairs chamber of the rebuilt Peter and Mary Whitmer Home. Joseph Smith and Oliver Cowdery spent the last month of Book of Mormon translation here. Photo by Casey Paul Griffiths.

Several members of the Whitmer family enjoyed special spiritual manifestations during the time that Joseph translated in their home. Revelations given to David, John, and Peter Whitmer Jr. now constitute sections 14, 15, and 16 of the Doctrine and Covenants. In revelation, David was told

243 Quoted in Lyndon W. Cook, ed., *David Whitmer Interviews: A Restoration Witness* (Orem, UT: Grandin Book Company, 1991), 233–34.

by the Lord: "If you keep my commandments and endure to the end you shall have eternal life, which gift is the greatest of all the gifts of God" (Doctrine and Covenants 14:7). John and Peter Jr. also received counsel from the Lord: "The thing which will be of the most worth unto you will be to declare repentance unto this people, that you may bring souls unto me" (Doctrine and Covenants 15:6; 16:6).

Spiritual manifestations were not limited to the men of the Whitmer family. Mary Whitmer, the matriarch of the family, became overwhelmed with taking care of her family's needs in addition to caring for Joseph Smith and Oliver Cowdery. In an 1878 interview with Joseph F. Smith, David Whitmer recounted: "My father and mother had a large family of their own, the addition to it therefore of Joseph, his wife Emma, and Oliver very greatly increased the toil and anxiety of my mother. And although she never complained she had sometimes felt that her labor was too much, or least she was beginning to feel so."[244] According to David, on a day during this time, Mary went out to the family barn to milk the family's cows, when she was met by an old man. The man said to her, "You have been very faithful and diligent in your labors, but you are tried because of the increase in your toil, it is proper therefore that you should receive a witness that your faith may be strengthened." The old man, whom David believed was the angel Moroni in disguise, then showed Mary the plates. David later recalled that the angel's appearance "completely removed all such feelings, and nerved her up for her increased responsibilities."[245] Depending on the timing of this event, it is possible that Mary was the first person besides Joseph to see the gold plates in person.

An important step towards the restoration of the priesthood also took place at the Whitmer farm. In a letter written near the end of his life, Joseph Smith listed some of the important early events of the Restoration, including a reference to "the voice of God in the chamber of old Father Whitmer" (Doctrine and Covenants 128:21).[246] Joseph wrote that he and Oliver Cowdery were anxious to know when they would receive the blessings of the Melchizedek Priesthood. He said they "had not long been engaged in solemn and fervent prayer, when the word of the Lord, came unto us in the Chamber, commanding us; that I should ordain Oliver Cowdery

244 "Report of Elders Orson Pratt and Joseph F. Smith."
245 "Report of Elders Orson Pratt and Joseph F. Smith."
246 "Letter to the Church, 7 September 1842 [D&C 128]," 7, JSP.

to be an Elder in the Church of Jesus Christ, and that he also should ordain me to the same office, and then <to> ordain others as it should be made known unto us, from time to time."[247]

After receiving this revelation, Joseph Smith stated: "We were however commanded to defer this our ordination until, such times, as it should be practicable to have our brethren, who had been and who should be baptized, assembled together, when we must have their sanction to our thus proceeding to ordain each other, and have them decide by vote whether they were willing to accept us as spiritual teachers, or not."[248] This instruction created the pattern in the restored Church of seeking a sustaining vote before ordaining or setting apart an individual as an officer of the Church. It also set the stage for the formal organization of the Church, which would take place at the Whitmer Farm several months later.

Mini-Devotional—"You Have Been Faithful and Diligent in Your Labors"

The spiritual experiences of the Whitmer family came to those who were directly involved in the work, such as David Whitmer, and those who served in supporting roles, such as Mary Whitmer. Although Mary did not assist in the translation, she labored diligently to make sure that everyone in the household was taken care of, and the Lord was aware of her efforts. The appearance of the angel to Mary shows the importance of those who might serve in lesser-known ways.

- Who are some people like Mary Whitmer who have offered support so that you could serve and grow spiritually?
- How can you show gratitude to the people who have supported you in your service?

247 Joseph Smith History, A-1, 27, JSP.
248 Joseph Smith History, A-1, 27, JSP.

The Three Witnesses at the Whitmer Farm

The Whitmer Home in early Summer. Photo by Casey Paul Griffiths.

While translating the Book of Mormon, Joseph Smith came across a verse that was written directly to him: "And behold, ye may be privileged that ye may show the plates unto those who shall assist to bring forth the work; and unto three shall they be shown by the power of God; wherefore they shall know of a surety that these things are true. And in the mouth of three witnesses shall these things be established" (Ether 5:2–4). Joseph had been commanded during his first meeting with the angel Moroni not to show the plates or the relics to anyone (Joseph Smith—History 1:42). He had stayed true to his promise, but this burden was overwhelming, and finally being able to share it with three others was a great relief. Near the end of the translation, Joseph gathered together a group of special witnesses at the Whitmer Farm to carry out this instruction found in the Book of Mormon.

Detail of the Three Witnesses panel on the Angel Moroni monument. Photo by Casey Paul Griffiths.

Before the sacred experience with the Three Witnesses, Joseph Smith sought instructions from the Lord about the role of the witnesses and what they would see. The resulting revelation, now Doctrine and Covenants 17, gave advice and counsel to the witnesses and listed the sacred objects they would be privileged to see. Reflecting on this revelation, Joseph wrote: "In the course of the work of translation, we ascertained that three special witnesses were to be provided by the Lord, to whom he would grant, that they should see the plates from which this work (the Book of Mormon) should be translated, and that these witnesses should bear record of the same; as will be found, recorded, [in the] Book of Mormon." He continued, "It occurred to Oliver Cowdery, David Whitmer, and the aforementioned Martin Harris (who had came to enquire after our progress in the work) that they would have me enquire of the Lord, to know if they might not obtain of him to be these three special witnesses; and finally they became so very solicitous, and teazed me so much, that at length <I> complied, and through the Urim and Thummin, I obtained of the Lord for them the folowing Revelation."[249]

249 Joseph Smith History, A-1, 23, JSP.

The Three Witnesses gathered at the Whitmer Farm in the summer of 1829 for their experience. In his 1838 history, Joseph Smith recorded what transpired as follows:

> Not many days after the above commandment [Doctrine and Covenants 17] was given, we four, viz Martin Harris, David Whitmer, Oliver Cowdery and myself, agreed to retire into the woods, and try to obtain by fervent and humble prayer, the fulfilment of the promises given in this revelation; that they should have a view of the pl[ates]. . . . We accordingly made choice of a piece of woods convenient to Mr. Whitmer's [house], to which we retired, and having knelt down, we began to pray in much faith, to Almighty God to bestow upon us a realization of those promises.[250]

The men each prayed, but they received no response. After several failed attempts, Martin Harris told the others that he believed he was stopping the others from receiving their promised manifestation, and he withdrew.

The remaining three engaged in prayer again. Joseph Smith recorded the experience that came soon after:

> We beheld a light above us in the air of exceeding brightness, and behold, an angel stood before us; in his hands he held the plates which we had been praying for these to have a view of: he turned over the leaves one by one, so that we could see them, and discern the engravings thereon distinctly: He addressed himself to David Whitmer, and said, "David, blessed is the Lord, and he that keeps his commandments:" when immediately afterwards we heard a voice from out of the bright light above us, saying "These plates have been revealed by the power of God, and they have been translated by the power of God; the translation of them which you have seen is correct, and I command you to bear record of what you now see and hear."[251]

After the experience, Joseph Smith left David Whitmer and Oliver Cowdery and went to find Martin Harris. Joseph said he found Martin

> at a considerable distance fervently engaged in prayer; he soon told me however that he had not yet prevailed with the Lord, and earnestly

250 Joseph Smith History, A-1, 24, JSP.
251 Joseph Smith History, A-1, 25, JSP.

> requested me, to join him in prayer, that he also might realize the same blessings which we had just received: we accordingly joined in prayer, and ultimately obtained our desires, for before we had yet finished, the same vision was opened to our view; at least it was again to me, and I once more beheld, and seen, and heard the same things; whilst at the same moment, Martin Harris cried out, apparently in an ecstasy of joy, "'Tis enough, 'tis enough; mine eyes have beheld, mine eyes have beheld," and jumping up he shouted, Hosanna, blessing God; and otherwise rejoiced exceedingly.[252]

Lucy Mack Smith, who was at the Whitmer Farm the day that the witnesses had their experience, later recorded:

> On coming in Joseph threw himself down beside me, and exclaimed; "Father, mother; you do not know [how] happy I am; the Lord has now caused the plates to be shown to three more besides myself.— they have seen an angel, who has testified to them; and they will have to bear witness to the truth of what I have said; for now they know for themselves, that I do not go about to deceive the people. And I feel as if I was relieved of a burden, which was almost to heavy for me to bear; and it rejoices my heart, that I am not any longer to be entirely alone in the world."[253]

Though all three of the witnesses eventually left the Church, none of them ever denied their testimony of the Book of Mormon or the events that took place at the Whitmer Farm. Oliver Cowdery was excommunicated from the Church in 1838, though he returned and was rebaptized in 1848, just before his passing in 1850. His widow, Elizabeth Whitmer Cowdery, affirmed that he never denied his witness. She said, "From the hour when the glorious vision of the Holy Messenger revealed to mortal eyes the hidden prophecies which God had promised his faithful followers should come forth in due time, until the moment when he passed away from earth. He always without one doubt or shudder of turning affirmed the divinity and truth of the Book of Mormon."[254]

---

252 Joseph Smith History, A-1, 25, JSP.

253 Lucy Mack Smith, History, 1845, 154, JSP.

254 Elizabeth Ann Cowdery to David Whitmer, March 8, 1887, in Larry E. Morris, *A Documentary History of the Book of Mormon* (New York: Oxford University Press, 2019), 396.

Martin Harris returned to the Church in 1870. His grave in Clarkson, Utah features the testimony of the Three Witnesses of the Book of Mormon. Photo by Kenneth Mays.

Martin Harris also left the Church in 1838. He remained affiliated with various breakoff groups before he rejoined the Church in 1870. Before his passing, Martin affirmed his testimony of the experience with the angel several times. William Pilkington, a young man who was hired to serve as a caretaker for Martin Harris, said he heard Martin share his testimony "scores of times." These occasions included a deathbed testimony given on the day before Martin died. During this last testimony, Martin asked William to hold up his right arm while he spoke. On another occasion, William recalled:

> His [Martin's] whole being became electrified and it seemed that a changed man stood before me . . . He said, 'Just as sure as you see the sun shining, just as sure am I that I stood in the presence of an Angel of God with Joseph Smith, and saw him hold the Gold Plates in his hands. I also saw the Urim and Thummim, the breastplate, and the sword of Laban. I saw the angel descend from heaven. The heavens were then opened and I heard the voice of God declare that everything the angel had told us was true, and that the Book of Mormon was translated correct[ly]. I was

commanded by God's voice to testify to the whole world what I had seen and heard."[255]

The headstone of David Whitmer in Richmond, Missouri, reads "The Record of the Jews and the Record of the Nephites are One. Truth is Eternal." Photo by Casey Paul Griffiths.

David Whitmer was excommunicated in 1838. He never returned to the Church. But David lived longer than any of the other witnesses and was interviewed more often than anyone else involved in the coming forth of the Book of Mormon. On several occasions, he described his experience with the plates in detail, saying:

> We not only saw the plates of the Book of Mormon, but also the Brass Plates, the plates of the Book of Ether, the plates containing the record of the wickedness and secret combinations of the people of the world down to the time of their being engraved, and many other plates. The fact is, it was just as though Oliver and I were sitting just here on the log,

255 William Pilkington Affidavit, April 3, 1934, 4–6, Church History Library, Salt Lake City, quoted in Morris, *Documentary History,* 402–3; spelling and punctuation corrected.

when we were overshadowed by a light. It was not like the light of the sun not like that of a fire, but more glorious and beautiful. It extended away round us, I cannot tell how far, but in the midst of this light about as far off as he sits (pointing to John C. Whitmer, sitting a few feet from him), there appeared, as it were, a table with many records or plates upon it, besides the plates of the Book of Mormon."[256]

Each of the witnesses faced serious persecution because of their testimonies. In one interview, David Whitmer recalled:

> I had a mob of from four to five hundred surrounding me at one time, demanding that I should deny my published statement in the Book of Mormon; but the testimony I bore the mob made them tremble before me. I heard the voice of the angel just as stated in said book, and the engravings on the plates were shown to us, and we were commanded to bear record of them; and if they are not true, then there is no truth, and if there is no truth there is no God; and if there is no God then there is no existence. But there is a God and I know it.[257]

The monument to the Three Witnesses is near the final resting place of Oliver Cowdery in Richmond, Missouri. Photo by Casey Paul Griffiths.

256 Quoted in Sidney B. Sperry, *Book of Mormon Compendium (Salt Lake City: Bookcraft, 1976),* 55–56.

257 James H. Hart interview, August 21, 1883, Richmond, Missouri, James H. Hart Notebook, in Cook, *David Whitmer Interviews,* 95–96.

The Organization of the Church

Interior of the rebuilt Whitmer home. Photo by Casey Paul Griffiths.

The culminating event of all the remarkable experiences on the Whitmer Farm came on April 6, 1830, when the Church was organized in the Whitmer home. As directed by revelation, Joseph Smith and Oliver Cowdery formally organized the Church with six original members. Though no list was produced the day the Church was organized, several later recollections help us know the identities of the founding six members. David Whitmer and Joseph Knight Sr., who were both members when the Church was organized, provided lists of those in attendance. Brigham Young also provided a list; although he joined the Church several years later, he was close with many of the members present at the organization. Each list included Joseph Smith Jr., Oliver Cowdery, and Hyrum Smith. Brigham's list, written around 1843, also included Samuel H. Smith, Joseph Smith Sr., and Orrin Porter Rockwell as founding members. Joseph Knight Sr. included Samuel H. Smith, Peter Whitmer Jr., and David Whitmer. David gave several lists, some including his brothers John Whitmer and Christian Whitmer. After analyzing all the evidence, historian Richard Lloyd Anderson concluded that the most likely list of the six founders is

Joseph Smith Jr., Oliver Cowdery, Hyrum Smith, David Whitmer, Peter Whitmer Jr., and Samuel H. Smith.[258]

Joseph Smith and Oliver Cowdery organized the Church as instructed by the Lord (see Doctrine and Covenants 21). Joseph described the first meeting of the newly organized Church as follows:

> Having opened the meeting by solemn prayer to our Heavenly Father we proceeded, (according to previous commandment) to call on our brethren to know whether they accepted us as their teachers in the things of the Kingdom of God, and whether they were satisfied that we should proceed and be organized as a Church according to said commandment which we had received. To these they consented by an unanimous vote. I then laid my hands upon Oliver Cowdery and ordained him an Elder of the "Church of Jesus Christ of Latter Day Saints." after which he ordained me also to the office of an Elder of said Church.[259]

This entry in Joseph's history was written after the official name of the Church was given in a revelation received in 1838 (Doctrine and Covenants 115:4), and Joseph retroactively used the official name in his history.

Further describing the meeting, the Prophet recorded: "We then took bread, blessed it, and brake it with them, also wine, blessed it, and drank it with them. We then laid our hands on each individual member of the Church present that they might receive the gift of the Holy Ghost, and be confirmed members of the Church of Christ. The Holy Ghost was poured out upon us to a very great degree. Some prophesied, whilst we all praised the Lord and rejoiced exceedingly."[260]

The original leadership of the Church on the day it was organized consisted simply of a first elder, Joseph Smith, and a second elder, Oliver Cowdery. Joseph and Oliver served as two unique witnesses of the Restoration: they were present at the restoration of the Aaronic Priesthood by John the Baptist (Doctrine and Covenants 13); they were ordained and confirmed as apostles by Peter, James, and John (Doctrine and Covenants 27:12); and they received priesthood keys in the Kirtland Temple from

---

258 "Who Were the Six Who Organized the Church on 6 April 1830?," *Ensign,* June 1980.

259 Joseph Smith History, A-1, 37, JSP.

260 Joseph Smith History, A-1, 37, JSP.

Moses, Elijah, and Elias (Doctrine and Covenants 110). On December 5, 1834, Joseph ordained Oliver "an assistant President of the High and Holy Priesthood."[261] After Oliver's excommunication in 1838, the Lord gave the role of second elder to Hyrum Smith. In a revelation given in 1841, the Lord directed that Hyrum "be crowned with the same blessing, and glory, and honor, and priesthood, and gifts of the priesthood, that once were put upon him that was [his] servant Oliver Cowdery" (Doctrine and Covenants 124:95).

Mini-Devotional—"Always Remember Him"

The Whitmer Farm was home to the first Church services in this dispensation. Sacred ordinances, such as the sacrament, took place here for the first time in these latter days. Today the Church serves as a home to millions of people, offering access to the redeeming power of Christ through these sacred ordinances. Take a moment to reflect on the following questions:

- How has the Church helped you progress in your life?
- What role do sacred ordinances like the sacrament play in helping you draw closer to God?

261 Joseph Smith, Journal, December 5, 1834, JSP.

The First Headquarters of the Church

The Whitmer Home served as the headquarters of the Church from April 1830 until January 1831. Photo by Casey Paul Griffiths.

For much of the first year following the Church's organization, the Whitmer Farm served as the Church headquarters. Because of increased persecution and opposition from Emma's family, Joseph and Emma Smith left their home in Harmony, Pennsylvania, and relocated to the Whitmer Farm in the fall of 1830. During his stay at the Whitmer Farm, Joseph received several key revelations that continued the Restoration. As the gospel spread, several key figures came to the Whitmer Farm to meet the Prophet in person. These visitors included Thomas B. Marsh, Parley P. Pratt, and Parley's brother Orson Pratt, who were all later ordained as apostles. In December 1830, Sidney Rigdon (later called as a counselor in the First Presidency) and Edward Partridge (later became the Church's first bishop) also visited the Whitmer Farm.

Even before Joseph Smith moved to the Whitmer Farm, trouble began brewing in his absence. The first signs of difficulty appeared in the weeks following the acceptance of the Articles and Covenants (Doctrine and Covenants 20) by the body of the Church. The Articles and Covenants were "received by the unanimous voice of the whole congregation" at a Church conference held on June 9, 1830.[262] A few weeks later, Oliver Cowdery sent a letter to Joseph Smith, ordering the Prophet to change part of the document. Oliver objected to the statement in the Articles and Covenants that before baptism, a candidate must "truly manifest by their works that they have received of the Spirit of Christ unto the remission of their sins" (Doctrine and Covenants 20:37). Oliver wrote to Joseph, saying: "I command you in the name of God to erase those words, that no priestcraft be amongst us."[263]

Alarmed at this message, Joseph wrote back to Oliver, asking "by what authority he took upon him to command [him] to alter, or erase, to add or diminish to or from a revelation or commandment from Almighty God." Joseph then traveled to Fayette, New York, where Oliver was staying with the Whitmer family, to discuss the issue. With the help of Christian Whitmer, Joseph persuaded Oliver and the Whitmers to relent in their efforts to change the document; however, Joseph noted that "it was not without both labor and perseverance that I could prevail with any of them to reason calmly on the subject."[264]

A few months later, in August 1830, a second challenge to the Prophet's leadership arose from the Whitmer family. Joseph and Emma Smith had moved from Harmony, Pennsylvania, to Fayette, New York. Upon their arrival, they found that Hiram Page, who was a brother-in-law to the Whitmer family and one of the Eight Witnesses of the Book of Mormon, "had got in his possession, a certain stone, by which he had obtained <two> revelations." Joseph later wrote that the revelations were "concerning the upbuilding of Zion [and] the order of the Church" and that they "were entirely at variance with the order of Gods house, as laid down in the new Testament, as well as in [their] late revelations."[265] Hiram suggested these revelations were binding upon the whole Church.

Newel Knight visited the Whitmer Farm during this time. "I found Brother Joseph in great trouble of mind on account of Hiram Page," wrote Newel. According to Newel, Hiram "had managed to bring some dissension

262 Minutes, June 9, 1830, JSP.
263 Joseph Smith History, A-1, 51, JSP.
264 Joseph Smith History, A-1, 51, JSP.
265 Joseph Smith History, A-1, 54, JSP.

of feeling among some of the brethren by pretending to revelation which he had got through the stone which were in direct contradiction to the New Testament and also to the revelations of God to us in these last days."[266] Emer Harris, another early Church member, recalled: "Bro. Hiram Page dug out of the earth a black stone [and] put it in his pocket. When he got home, he looked at it. It contained a sentence on paper to befit it. As soon as he wrote one sentence, another sentence came on the stone, until he wrote 16 pages."[267]

After counseling with other Church members, Joseph Smith decided to settle the matter at a conference planned for September 1, 1830. He later wrote, "I thought it wisdom not to do much more than to converse with the brethren on the subject, untill the conference should meet. Finding however that many (especially the Whitmer family and Oliver Cowdery) were believing much in the things set forth by this stone, we thought best to enquire of the Lord concerning so important a matter."[268] The revelation that the Prophet received, now Doctrine and Covenants 28, addressed the tensions in the Church. The Lord specified that while anyone in the Church could receive personal revelation, "no one shall be appointed to receive commandments and revelations in this church excepting [his] servant Joseph Smith, Jun., for he receiveth them even as Moses" (Doctrine and Covenants 28:2).

This direction from the Lord established the principle of revelation based on stewardship, which is still in the Church today. While personal revelation flows freely to all God's children, revelation for others comes based on a person's stewardship. A bishop receives revelation for his ward, a Relief Society president receives revelation for the sisters in her charge, and a father and mother receive revelation together for their family. After the revelation, the Whitmer family accepted the principles, and Hiram Page gave up his seer stone. One witness later recalled that the stone was "broke to powder and the writings burnt."[269] Newel Knight remembered that "all

266 Michael Hubbard Mackay and William H. Hartley, eds., *The Rise of the Latter-day Saints: The Journals and Histories of Newel Knight (Provo, UT: Brigham Young University Religious Studies Center; Salt Lake City: Deseret Book Company,* 2019), 21.

267 Emer Harris, Provo Utah Central Stake General Minutes, April 6, 1856, vol. 10, 273.

268 Joseph Smith History, A-1, 54, JSP.

269 Emer Harris, Provo Utah Central Stake General Minutes, 273.

the members of the Church present renounced the stone, and the revelations connected with it, much to [their] joy and satisfaction."[270]

The revelation also provided the first clue to the location of the city of Zion. The Lord told the Church, "No man knoweth where the city Zion shall be built, but it shall be given hereafter. Behold I say unto you that it shall be on the borders by the Lamanites" (Doctrine and Covenants 28:9). The Lord commanded Oliver Cowdery to organize the first official mission of the Church to travel to the boundaries of the United States. A later revelation instructed Parley P. Pratt, Ziba Peterson, and Peter Whitmer Jr. to accompany Oliver on his journey to the border by the Lamanites (Doctrine and Covenants 32). The "Lamanite missionaries" set out in the fall of 1830, playing an instrumental role in gathering hundreds of converts in the regions around Kirtland, Ohio. The missionaries eventually arrived at Independence, Missouri, which the Lord identified as the location of the city of Zion (Doctrine and Covenants 57:1–2).

Visitors to the Whitmer Farm

As missionaries departed from the Whitmer Farm, new and enthusiastic converts gathered to the farm, seeking revelation and guidance from the Prophet. Thomas B. Marsh (later called as President of the Quorum of the Twelve) attended a conference held at the Whitmer Farm in September 1830. At the conference, Joseph Smith received a revelation for him. The Lord told Thomas, "You have had many afflictions because of your family; nevertheless, I will bless you and your family, yea, your little ones; and that day cometh that they will believe and know the truth and be one with you in my church" (Doctrine and Covenants 31:2). Thomas and his entire family were baptized into the Church around the time this revelation was given.

270 "Newel Knight's Journal," in *Scraps of Biography: Tenth Book of the Faith-Promoting Series: Designed for the Instruction and Encouragement of Young Latter-day Saints*, ed. Juvenile Instructor Office (Salt Lake City, 1883), 65.

Engraving of Orson Pratt. Courtesy Church History Library.

Another visitor to the Whitmer Farm was future apostle Orson Pratt, who was converted by his brother Parley P. Pratt. Orson arrived at the farm in November 1830. It was during this visit that Joseph Smith received a revelation for Orson (Doctrine and Covenants 34). An acquaintance of Orson later recorded a secondhand account of what it was like to receive a revelation through the Prophet. He wrote that Orson

> was anxious to know what his mission was and would be, and at Peter Whitmer Sr's residence he asked Joseph whether he could not ascertain what his mission was, and Joseph answered him that he would see, & asked Pratt and John Whitmer to go upstairs with him, and on arriving there Joseph produced a small stone called a seer stone, and putting it into a Hat soon commenced speaking and asked Elder P[ratt] to write as he would speak, but being too young and timid and feeling his unworthiness he asked whether Bro. John W[hitmer] could not write it, and the Prophet said that he could: Then came the revelation [Doctrine and Covenants 34].[271]

In the revelation, Orson was called as a missionary, with the Lord telling him to "lift up [his] voice as with the sound of a trump, both long and loud, and cry repentance unto a crooked and perverse generation, preparing the way of the Lord for his second coming" (Doctrine and Covenants 34:6).

In December 1830, two more visitors arrived at the Whitmer Farm: Sidney Rigdon and his friend Edward Partridge. Sidney and Edward were both converted to the gospel in Ohio by the Lamanite missionaries who had departed from the Whitmer Farm a few months earlier. Sidney was a

271 James R. B. Van Cleave to Joseph Smith III, Richmond, September 29, 1878, Community of Christ Library and Archives, Independence, Missouri.

prominent Campbellite minister in Ohio, and he left his Church when he became convinced of the truth of the Book of Mormon. After long discussions with the missionaries, particularly Parley P. Pratt and Oliver Cowdery, Sidney saw a vision. He later wrote,

> I saw the different orders of professing Christians passing before my eyes, with their hearts, exposed to view, and they were as corrupt as corruption itself. That society to which I belonged [the Reformed Baptists] also passed before my eyes, and to my astonishment it was as corrupt as the others. Last of all *that little man* who [brought] me the Book of Mormon [Oliver Cowdery], passed before my eyes with his heart open, and it was as pure as an angel; and this was a testimony from God; that the Book of Mormon was a Divine Revelation.[272]

A few weeks after his baptism, Sidney Rigdon traveled to New York with Edward Partridge. Both were determined and anxious to meet with the Prophet who had brought forth the Book of Mormon. Shortly after Sidney and Edward arrived at the Whitmer Farm, Joseph Smith received a revelation on behalf of Sidney (Doctrine and Covenants 35). The revelation commended Sidney for his work as a minister, telling him: "Thou wast sent forth, even as John [the Baptist], to prepare the way before me" (Doctrine and Covenants 35:4). The Lord also commanded Sidney to assist Joseph in his translation of the Bible, saying: "Thou shalt write from him; and the scriptures shall be given" (Doctrine and Covenants 35:20).

Edward Partridge came to the Whitmer Farm with heavy questions weighing on his mind. Two years earlier, Edward and his wife, Lydia Partridge, had been members of Sidney Rigdon's movement. Edward was working as a successful hatter in Painesville, Ohio, when he received word that a group of missionaries who claimed to carry a new book of scripture had arrived in the area. According to Lydia, when the four missionaries arrived at their home, Edward told them that they were imposters, but "Oliver Cowdery replied that he was thankful there was a God in Heaven who knew the hearts of all men." Oliver's statement implied that he believed Edward was an honest man who would eventually accept the gospel. Edward, intrigued by the missionaries' message despite his abrupt

272 Cited in Eber Howe, *Mormonism Unveiled* (Painesville, OH, 1834), 246–47.

comments, quickly sent one of his employees to obtain a copy of the new book they carried with them.[273]

Lydia Partridge was baptized a short time later, though Edward Partridge remained unsure about whether he should join the new religion. Edward had been touched by the missionaries' message but decided he would not be baptized until he could speak with Joseph Smith face-to-face. He decided to travel with Sidney Rigdon to New York to meet the Prophet. According to Philo Dibble, another new convert from the area, Edward went not only for himself but on behalf of others in Painesville, Ohio, who were interested in the new church. This group of seekers even helped pay part of Edward's expenses for the trip and chose him to be the messenger because he was "a man who would not lie [to save] his right arm."[274]

Regarding the first meeting of Sidney Rigdon and Edward Partridge with Joseph Smith, Lucy Mack Smith wrote:

> Joseph came with his wife again to Waterloo and appointed a meeting at our house. While he was preaching, Sidney Rigdon and Edward Partridge came in. After the sermon, a request was made that any who felt to speak should make <such> remarks as occurred to their minds. Mr. Partridge arose and stated that he had been to Manchester in se[a]rch of us to ascertain the truth of what we preached that he had visit[ed] some of our neighbors in that place and enquired the character of the family some they said that the Smith family were very [r]espectable people and no one could say ought against them until Joseph deceived them about the plates He had also walked over our farm and seen the neatness, order and industry exhibited in everything around he had seen what we had sacrificed for the truth's sake and yet our enemies did not dispute our veracity upon any point but that of religion.[275]

Lucy continued, "[Edward then said,] 'I am ready to be baptized, Brother Joseph will you baptize me?' . . . [Joseph replied,] 'You have traveled a long way this morning, and you are much fatigued, and I think you had better rest and take some refreshment and tomorrow morning be baptized.'

273 Scott H. Partridge, "Edward Partridge in Painesville, Ohio," *BYU Studies Quarterly* 42, no. 1 (2003): 56.

274 Partridge, "Edward Partridge in Painesville, Ohio," 56.

275 Lucy Mack Smith, History, 1844–1845, bk. 10 [11], The Joseph Smith Papers, July 8, 2022, https://www.josephsmithpapers.org/paper-summary/lucy-mack-smith-history-1844-1845/123.

'Just as you think proper,' replied Mr. Partridge, 'I am ready.'"[276] Shortly after this conversation, Joseph dictated a revelation on behalf of Edward (Doctrine and Covenants 36). In the revelation, the Lord told Edward: "You are blessed, and your sins are forgiven you, and you are called to preach my gospel as with the sound of a trump" (Doctrine and Covenants 36:1). Despite the cold weather, Joseph baptized Edward in the Seneca River on December 11, 1830. Three days following the baptism, as mentioned in the revelation, Sidney ordained him an elder.

Sidney Rigdon insisted on seeing Joseph Smith after missionaries converted him. Photo courtesy Church History Library.

Engraving of Edward Partridge. Courtesy Church History Library.

The arrival of Sidney Rigdon and Edward Partridge demonstrated that the Lord was beginning the work of spreading the gospel to all nations, but it also marked the beginning of the end of the Whitmer Farm acting as Church headquarters. Soon after Sidney and Edward arrived in Fayette, New York, Joseph Smith received a revelation commanding the members of the Church to "assemble together at the Ohio" (Doctrine and Covenants

276 Lucy Mack Smith, History, 1844–1845, bk. 10 [11], The Joseph Smith Papers, July 8, 2022, https://www.josephsmithpapers.org/paper-summary/lucy-mack-smith-history-1844-1845/123; punctuation and capitalization corrected.

37:3). The Lord promised, "There I will give unto you my law; and there you shall be endowed with power from on high" (Doctrine and Covenants 38:32). Joseph and Emma Smith departed the Whitmer Farm to move to Kirtland, Ohio, in February 1831. A few months later, the Whitmer family sold the farm and departed for Ohio as well, with many family members eventually moving on to Missouri to build the city of Zion on the frontier.

In 1926, Elder B. H. Roberts purchased 120 acres in New York on behalf of the Church, regaining ownership of the Whitmer Farm. The original location of the Whitmer Farm was determined in 1946–47, and in 1979 the Church constructed the first replica of the Peter Whitmer Sr. cabin. Spencer W. Kimball dedicated the site on April 6, 1980, to commemorate the 150th anniversary of the organization of the Church.[277]

The chapel at the Whitmer farm was built in preparation for the 150th anniversary of the founding of the Church. Photo by Casey Paul Griffiths.

Though the Peter Whitmer Senior Farm served as Church headquarters for less than a year, the importance of the events that took place there is immeasurable. The Prophet Joseph Smith found sanctuary with the Whitmer family when he most needed it, and in turn, the Whitmers were repaid through rich spiritual experiences. More revelations were received in the Whitmer home than in any other single place in the history of the Church.

277 "Peter Whitmer, Sr. Home, Fayette, New York," Ensign Peak Foundation, accessed June 14, 2022, https://ensignpeakfoundation.org/peter-whitmer-sr-farm-home/.

Mini-Devotional—"He Receiveth Them, Even as Moses"

At the Whitmer Farm, the early members of the Church worked out many of the principles we take for granted today. Revelation, stewardship, and prophetic guidance provided great strength to the men and women of the early Church. The Lord freely provided guidance through inspired revelation, counsel from Church leaders, and scriptural wisdom to help establish the foundations of His Church. Reflect on these events as you answer the following questions:

- How have you received revelation in your own life?
- Why is it important to confirm our personal revelation with counsel from Church leaders and from the scriptures?

Take a moment to share or write down your testimony on the importance of revelation and guidance from inspired sources.

Significant events at this location . . .

- Joseph and Emma Smith made their first home together at this site, living here from 1828 to 1830.
- The majority of the translation of the Book of Mormon took place at this location.
- John the Baptist appeared near this location and bestowed the priesthood of Aaron on Joseph Smith and Oliver Cowdery (Doctrine and Covenants 13).
- Near this location Peter, James, and John appeared and "committed the keys of my kingdom, and a dispensation of the gospel for the last times" (Doctrine and Covenants 27:13, 128:20).
- Emma Smith gave birth to her first child, Alvin Smith, at this location and the grave marker for the child is found in the nearby cemetery.
- Doctrine and Covenants 3, 4, 5, 6, 7, 8, 9, 10, 11, 12, 13, 24, 25, 26, 27 were received at or near this location.

THE RESTORATION OF THE PRIESTHOOD

The Priesthood Restoration Site

The Priesthood Restoration site is located near present-day Susquehanna, Pennsylvania. Photo by Casey Paul Griffiths.

Located near the present-day town on Oakland, Pennsylvania is the Priesthood Restoration site. During the early 19th century the location was known as Harmony. Harmony was the hometown of Emma Hale and the place where she and her new husband, Joseph Smith, first made their home in 1827. It was at this location where a large portion of the Book of Mormon was translated, and several angelic beings appeared to Joseph Smith and Oliver Cowdery to restore priesthood authority to the earth. Among the angels who appeared near this location are John the Baptist (Doctrine and Covenants 13), Peter, James, John (Doctrine and Covenants 128:20), and Moroni.[278] Even Michael the Archangel engaged visited this area to assist in the work of restoration (Doctrine and Covenants 128:20).

A new chapel which houses the visitor's center was dedicated in 2015. In addition the Isaac Hale home was rebuilt along with the cabin Joseph and Emma lived in during their time here. There are curated paths all throughout the site for visitors. Just down the road there is a small walkway down to the banks of the Susquehanna river. Visitors to the Priesthood Restoration Site should park at the church building and check-in with the missionaries there for tours of the properties.

The First Home of Joseph and Emma Smith

The rebuilt home of Joseph and Emma Smith. Much of the translation of the Book of Mormon took place here. Photo by Casey Paul Griffiths.

In October 1825 Joseph Smith was hired by a man named Josiah Stowell to travel to Harmony, Pennsylvania in pursuit of rumors of an old Spanish silver mine. The occurred shortly after Alvin Smith's death when he

278 See Joseph Smith History, vol. A-1, 10, JSP.

family was struggling financially. Joseph's mother recalled, "[Stowell] came for Joseph from having heard, that he was in possession of certain means, by which he could discern things, that could not be seen by the natural eye. Joseph endeavored to divert him from his vain project; but he was inflexible, and offered high wages to such as would dig for him; and was still very anxious to have Joseph work for him."[279] Joseph remembered, "I continued to work for nearly a month, without success in our undertaking, and finally I prevailed with the old gentleman to cease digging after it. Hence arose the very prevalent story of my having been a money-digger" (Joseph Smith-History 1:56).

One successful byproduct of Joseph's venture with Josiah Stowell was his acquaintance with Emma Hale. Joseph boarded with the Hale family during his time in Harmony. Emma was a year older than Joseph, and their courtship caused some concern in the Hale family. Isaac Hale later said, "[The] young Smith made several visits at my house, and at length asked my consent to marry my daughter Emma. This I refused, and gave my reasons for so doing; some of which were, that he was a stranger, and followed a business that I could not approve; he then left the place. Not long after this, he returned, and while I was absent from home, carried off my daughter, in the state of New York, where they were married without my approbation or consent."[280]

In 1838, in a series of questions and answers published in the *Elder's Journal*, Joseph Smith commented on the circumstances surrounding his marriage. When asked, "Did not Jo Smith steal his wife[?]," Joseph replied simply, "Ask her; she was of age, she can answer for herself."[281] In an interview carried out by her son Joseph Smith III near the end of her life, Emma commented on her side of the story: "I had no intention of marrying when I left home; but, during my visit at Mr. Stowell's, your father visited me there. My folks were bitterly opposed to him; and, being importuned by your father, aided by Mr. Stowell, who urged me to marry him, and preferring to marry him to any other man I knew, I consented. We went to Squire [Zachariah] Tarbell's and were married."[282]

---

279 "Lucy Mack Smith, History, 1845," p. 95, The Joseph Smith Papers, accessed March 21, 2022, https://www.josephsmithpapers.org/paper-summary/lucy-mack-smith-history-1845/102

280 Larry E. Morris, *A Documentary History of the Book of Mormon,* 2019, 82.

281 "Questions and Answers, 8 May 1838," p. 43, JSP.

282 Last Testimony of Sister Emma," Saints' Herald, Oct. 1, 1879, 289.

The First Phase of the Translation of the Book of Mormon: Winter-Spring 1828

Because of intense persecution in Joseph's hometown of Palmya, the young couple chose to leave the area and travel Harmony, nearer to Emma's family. During the journey to Harmony, Joseph hid the plates in a barrel of beans. Joseph's friend Orson Pratt wrote about a confrontation that happened during their trip: "He had not gone far, before he was overtaken by an officer with a search-warrant, who flattered himself with the idea, that he should surely obtain the plates; after searching very diligently, he was sadly disappointed at not finding them." Further along the road, another confrontation occurred, "[Joseph] was again overtaken by an officer on the same business, and after ransacking the wagon very carefully, he went his way, as much chagrined as the first, at not being able to discover the object of his research. Without any further molestation, he pursued his journey until he came into the northern part of Pennsylvania, near the Susquehanna river, in which part his father-in-law resided."[283]

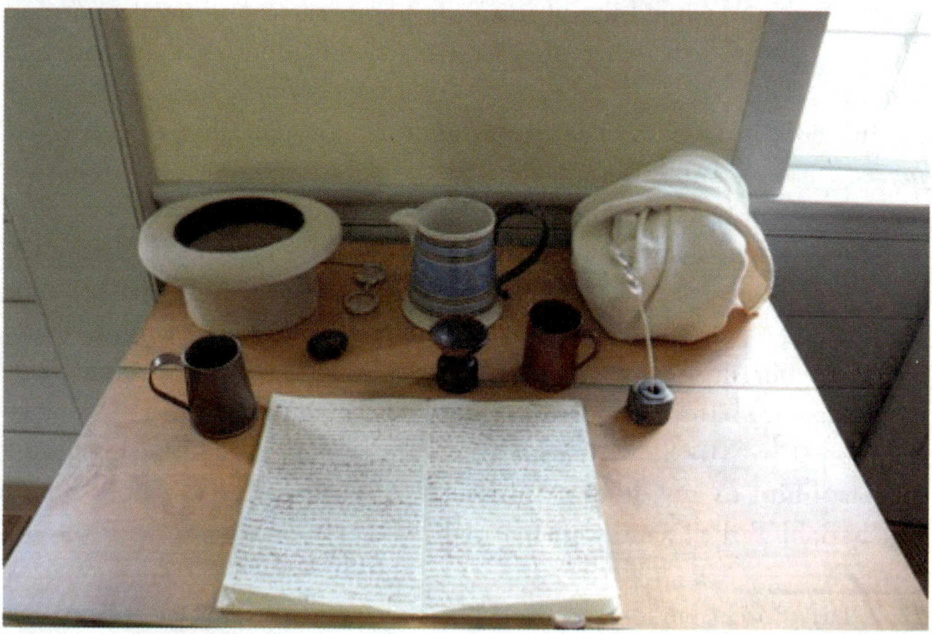

Interior of the JOseph and Emma Smith home shows what some of the instruments of translation my have looked like. Photo by Casey Paul Griffiths.

283 Orson Pratt, *An Interesting Account of Several Remarkable Visions,* Edinburgh, United Kingdom, (1840) 13–14.

Because of the circumstances of their marriage, their relationship with Emma's family was still tentative. After they arrived in the area, the couple worked to reconcile the Hale family to their marriage and Joseph's prophetic work. They even went so far as to allow Emma's father, Isaac, to handle plates while they were contained in a box. Isaac Hale later reported, "I was informed they had brought a wonderful book of Plates down with them. I was shown a box in which it is said they were contained, which had to all appearances been used as a glass box of common window glass. I was allowed to feel the weight of the box, and they gave me to understand, that the plates was then in the box—into which, however, I was not allowed to look."[284] Isaac remained skeptical of Joseph's work.

Martin Harris Departs From Harmony to Find the Three Wise Men

One of Joseph's most important friends was Martin Harris, who soon visited Harmony. Martin helped Joseph and Emma pay for their move to Harmony and spent much of the winter of 1827-28 here, assisting as one of the early scribes of the Book of Mormon. Joseph's 1832 history notes that because of Martin's assistance "the Lord appeared unto [Martin] in vision and showed him the his marvelous work which he was about to do." When Martin arrived in Harmony in February 1828 he told Joseph that "the Lord had shown him that he must go to New York City with some of the characters" on the plates. Joseph demonstrated his truth in Martin by copying some of the characters onto a piece of paper that he gave to Martin before he set out on his journey east.[285]

While Charles Anthon, prominent scholar in New York City, is the figure who receives the most attention in this story, contemporary sources indicate that Martin called on several other scholars during his trip. Pomeroy Tucker, a Palmyra citizen, wrote that Martin sought out "the interpretation and bibliographical scrutiny of such scholars as Hon. Luther Bradish, Dr.

284 Larry E. Morris, *A Documentary History of the Book of Mormon*, 82.

285 Joseph Smith History, circa Summer 1832, 5, JSP.

[Samuel] Mitchell, Prof. Anthon and others."[286] One historian later jokingly referred to these three scholars as "the three wise men of the east."[287]

The first of the wise men, Luther Bradish, used to live in Palmyra, increasing the chances that he and Martin knew each other. By the time Martin visited, Bradish was a successful Wall Street lawyer and a New York State assemblyman. Bradish also spent time in Egypt as an agent for the American government. Martin may have seen him a possible source of expertise, or at least someone who might know someone with knowledge about Egyptian hieroglyphics. We know very little about their meeting, though they probably met in Albany, New York. Bradish was serving there in the legislature in February 1828. During their meeting, Bradish probably referred Martin to another scholar in New York City, Professor Samuel L. Mitchill, one of the country's leading naturalists.[288]

Martin then traveled to New York City, where he met with Mitchill, a man known among his colleagues as the "nestor of American science," a "stalking library," and "the Delphic oracle of New York." Mitchill in turn referred Martin to an upcoming young scholar of linguistics, Charles Anthon. Anthon was an impressive specialist in Greek, Latin, German, and French, there remain few indications that he knew much about Egyptian, Hebrew, or any other Middle Eastern language. Though the encounter convinced Martin that the characters were genuine, in letters written in 1834 and 1841 Anthon disputed Martin's account of their meeting, though he contradicted himself in the way he told the story in each letter. In the 1834 letter, Anthon said that Martin "intended selling his farm and giving the amount to those who wished to publish the plates," while in the 1841 letter Anthon stated that Martin left his office determined not to sell his farm "or embark in the speculation of printing the golden book."[289]

Charles Anthon became the most prominent of the three wise men because of his mention in Joseph Smith's history. Out of the three scholars, we know the most about the meeting he had with Martin Harris. When Joseph Smith translated Isaiah's prophecy in 2 Nephi 27:15–18, he was convinced that the learned man in it was a reference to Charles Anthon.[290] Regardless

286 Morris, *A Documentary History of the Book of Mormon,* 246.

287 Richard E. Bennett, "Read This, I Pray Thee: Martin Harris and the Three Wise Men of the East," *Journal of Mormon History,* 36:1, 2010,184–89.

288 Bennett, "Read This, I Pray Thee," 184-189.

289 Bennett, "Read This, I Pray Thee," 190–93.

290 MacKay and Dirkmaat, *From Darkness Into Light*, 52.

of the disputes over what was said between the two men, one fact is indisputable—Martin returned from his trip to the East to Harmony convinced that the characters were genuine and could be translated only through divine revelation from God.

The Translation of the Book of Mormon

Even while Martin was holding his meetings with three scholars, Joseph continued to labor on the translation of the Book of Mormon. A large share of the translation took place in Joseph and Emma's home in Harmony. From the first edition of the Book of Mormon published in 1830 to the present, every copy has included a statement from Joseph Smith that the text of the book was "translated by the gift and power of God." In reference to the process, the term *translation* has been widely utilized as a catch-all description of how the book was produced, though the process was very different from any traditional form of translation. The translation of the Book of Mormon was a miracle, but the details come from a number of different witnesses who participated in the translation in varied ways. In their recollections, all of these witnesses sought to emphasize the supernatural nature of the process. The sacred objects present during the translation—the Nephite Interpreters, the Liahona, the Sword of Laban, and most notably the plates themselves—are no longer in the hands of mortals. One instrument likely used in the translation, the brown seer stone, is still found on earth.

The brown stone was one of several instruments used in the translation. Joseph Smith and his associates often spoke of "interpreters" buried alongside the plates as one of the tools used to receive the text. In the Book of Mormon, the prophet Moroni spoke of having "sealed up the interpreters, according to the commandment of the Lord" (Ether 4:5). Martin Harris described the interpreters as "two stones set in a bow of silver . . . about two inches in diameter, perfectly round." He continued, "The stones were white, like polished marble, with a few gray streaks." Lucy Mack Smith gave a similar account, describing the interpreters as "2 smooth 3 cornered diamonds set in glass and the glass was set in silver bows connected with each other in the same way that old fashioned spectacles are made."

Both the Nephite interpreters and the seer stone were used in the translation. In her recollections, Emma Smith explained that Joseph began translating "by use of Urim and Thummim, and that portion of the translation was the part that Martin Harris lost. *After that he used a small stone,* not exactly black, but was rather a dark color." Sources from the time indicate that Joseph Smith owned more than one seer stone, though evidence generally points to the brown seer stone as the instrument used in translation. It can be difficult to determine which instruments were used during the translation process, since both are referred to as *interpreters* or described through the use of the biblical term *Urim and Thummim* by participants in the translation process.

Photo of the brown seerstone first published by the Joseph Smith Papers in 2015. Courtesy Joseph Smith Papers.

When it comes to the use of the brown stone in translation several participants described how the stone was used. Emma Smith, who served as scribe while she and Joseph were living in Harmony, Pennsylvania, said that she "frequently wrote day after day" and described Joseph "sitting with his face buried in his hat, with the stone in it, and dictating hour after hour with nothing between us." When Emma was asked to share her testimony of the translation process near the end of her life, she said, "The Book of Mormon is of divine authenticity—I have not the slightest doubt of it. I am satisfied that no man could have dictated the writing of the manuscripts unless he was inspired; for, when acting as his scribe, your father would dictate to me for hour after hour; and when returning after meals, or after interruptions, he would at once begin where he left off, without either seeing the manuscript or having any portion of it read to him."[291]

We may never know all of the exact details of the translation process of the Book of Mormon, but it is important to keep in mind that translation was a supernatural process, aided by the power of God. The use of seer stone or other divine instruments in another example of the miracle of ancient days returning to bring about the "marvelous work and a wonder" prophesied for the latter days. In ancient times prophets used physical objects like the Rod of Aaron (Exodus 7:12), a Brass Serpent (Numbers 21:8), or sacred arks (Joshua 3:15) to mediate divine power. In our time sacred anointing oil, common bread, and water are used for the same purposes. In Joseph Smith's time, seer stones and divine interpreters played a vital role in allowing the Prophet and his associates to translate "by the gift and power of God."

During this early phase of the translation, Martin Harris and Emma Smith acted as the primary scribes. The work from this early phase of translation was lost, however, when Martin Harris took the manuscript home to Palmyra. A large part of the reason why the worked ceased came because Emma Smith was about to give birth to their first child. Unfortunately, the child died a few hours after birth, and Emma almost died as well. The child, named after Joseph's deceased brother Alvin, is buried in the McKune Cemetery just up the hill from where Joseph and Emma's cabin is located. The grave marker has been preserved and reads, "In memory of an infant son of Joseph and Emma Smith June 15th 1828." The grave is near the edge of the cemetery near the trees and is not difficult to find. It was placed in a granite marker to preserve it. Nearby are the graves of Emma's parents, Isaac and Elizabeth are nearby.

The devastating loss of the manuscript, along with the death of their first child, caused Joseph and Emma to pause the work for several months. Joseph spent the summer farming, and only translated sporadically throughout the Fall and Winter of 1828. There may have been a crisis of confidence with these heartbreaking setbacks. But in the Spring of 1829, a visitor arrived at Joseph and Emma's cabin who lit the fire that fulfilled the coming forth of the record.

---

291 "Last Testimony of Sister Emma," *Saint's Herald,* vol. 26, no. 19, 289.

The Second Phase of the Translation of the Book of Mormon: Spring-Summer 1829

The Joseph and Emma Smith home. When Oliver Cowdery arrived here in April 1829 the second phase of translation began. Photo by Casey Paul Griffiths.

On April 5, 1829, a sabbath-day evening, Oliver Cowdery and Samuel H. Smith arrived in Harmony. Oliver became acquainted with the Smiths when he moved to Palmyra the previous Fall. Boarding with the Smith family, he was told about the plates and Joseph Smith's prophetic call. Meanwhile in Harmony, Joseph was struggling to begin again on the translation. Lucy Mack Smith later recalled, "Joseph has been so hurried with his secular affairs, that he could not proceed with his spiritual concerns so fast as was necessary for the speedy completion of the work." Emma acted as a scribe when she was able, but she "had so much of her time taken up with the care of the house, that she could write for but a small portion of the time."[292]

292 Lucy Mack Smith History, 1844–1845, bk. 8, 4, JSP.

Lucy Mack Smith recalled, "Joseph called upon the Lord, three days prior to the arrival of Samuel and Oliver, to send him a scribe, according to the promise of the angel; and he was informed that the same should be forthcoming in a few days. Accordingly, when Mr. Cowdery told him the business he had come upon, Joseph was not at all surprised."[293] Shortly after Oliver arrived, Doctrine and Covenants 6 was received on his behalf. The precise date of this revelation is unknown, but it appears to have been shortly after Oliver arrived in Harmony. Immediately Joseph and Oliver forged a friendship and launched a new phase of the translation. In an 1834 letter to W. W. Phelps, Oliver notes that he arrived in Harmony on April 5 and then commenced his work as scribe of the translation just two days later, on April 7, 1829.[294]

In addition to Doctrine and Covenants 6, several revelations came shortly after Oliver's arrival. These revelations (Doctrine and Covenants 7-9) contain some of the best insights into the spiritual nature of the translation process, and personal revelation in general. Joseph Smith later wrote, "Whilst continuing the work of translation during the month of April; Oliver Cowdery became exceedingly anxious to have the power to translate bestowed upon him."[295] Oliver was told earlier by the Lord, "I grant unto you a gift, if thou desire of me, to translate, even as my servant Joseph" (D&C 6:25). After Oliver expressed his desire to translate, Joseph sought the Lord and recorded the revelation now known as Doctrine and Covenants 8. This revelation and Doctrine and Covenants 7 and 9 were all received around the same time. While in every published version of the Doctrine and Covenants the revelation in section 8 has been placed after the revelation about John the Beloved, there is some question of when it was received. In the earliest compilation, John Whitmer, the first Church historian, placed this revelation before Doctrine and Covenants 7.[296] Doctrine and Covenants 8 is another crucial stepping-stone in Oliver's introduction to the process of receiving revelation from God. In Joseph Smith's official history, Doctrine and Covenants 9 appears directly after section 8 without any explanation or introduction.[297] It is clear from the text of the revelation that Oliver attempted to translate but was ultimately unsuccessful.

293 Lucy Mack Smith History, 1844–1845, bk. 8, 4, JSP

294 "Letter I," *Latter-day Saints' Messenger and Advocate,* October 1834, 1:13–16.

295 History, 1838–1856, vol. A-1, 16.

296 Revelation Book 1, 12, JSP.

297 History, 1838–1856, vol. A-1, 17.

The Lord takes time to tenderly explain to Oliver why he was unable to translate.

The sequence of these revelations show the Lord's willingness to provide answers and guidance to sincere seekers. In Doctrine and Covenants 7, Joseph and Oliver learned of a blessings granted to John the Beloved when the Lord sense his desires. The Savior blessed John to be "I will make him as flaming fire and a ministering angel; he shall minister for those who shall be heirs of salvation who dwell on the earth" (Doctrine and Covenants 7:6). Learning how John's request was granted may have led Oliver to inquire about his own secret desire. He wanted to translate the way Joseph did. The Savior gave Oliver permission to translate. His counsel to Oliver suggests that the translation process was more than just simply writing down the words appearing in the instruments. The Savior taught Oliver, "behold, I will tell you in your mind and in your heart, by the Holy Ghost, which shall come upon you and which shall dwell in your heart. Now, behold, this is the spirit of revelation" (Doctrine and Covenants 8:2-3).

Based on the content of Doctrine and Covenants 9, it appears that Oliver was unable to translate. This revelation was given in response to Oliver's frustrations. The Lord lovingly counsels Oliver that there is more to the process of revelation that simply asking. "Behold, you have not understood; you have supposed that I would give it unto you, when you took no thought save it was to ask me. But, behold, I say unto you, that you must study it out in your mind; then you must ask me if it be right" (Doctrine and Covenants 9:7-8). Oliver was taught that revelation from God must involve work on the behalf of the seeker. We must do all the work we can to be prepared for the revelation, make our decision, and then inquire of the Lord. With the pressing need to complete the translation, Oliver returned to his work as a scribe but with the Savior's promise that he would receive power to assist in the coming forth of other sacred records (Doctrine and Covenants 9:2).

Mini-Devotional: "This is the Spirit of Revelation."

Oliver's experiences with translation show the Lord's tutoring in the process of revelation. For instance, the in first revelation given to him he was told that he had already received a revelation. The Lord told him "cast your mind upon the night that you cried unto me in your heart, that you might know concerning the truth of these things" (Doctrine and Covenants 8:22). The speaks to us all the time, but we sometimes don't recognize the revelation when it comes.

- Have you ever had an experience that you realized later was God speaking to you?

The next lesson that Oliver was taught was that anyone could come to the Lord with their heart's desires and ask in faith. Sometimes the request was granted, as in the request John the Beloved made of the Savior. It can be even more difficult when we don't get answers right away, or don't get the answers we wanted. Oliver took no thought except to ask the Lord for his answers, and was taught that he played a role in receiving the revelation he desired.

- Why is it important to put in the effort needed to receive a revelation?
- When has effort made a difference in receiving personal revelation?
- Share an experience about a time you received a personal revelation? How did you come to know it was a revelation, and what effort did you put in to receive it?

The Appearance of John the Baptist

Aaronic Priesthood restoration monument at the Priesthood Restoration site. Photo by Casey Paul Griffiths.

One of the reasons why Harmony is such a sacred place is the appearance of angels, including John the Baptist. Monuments to the appearance of John the Baptist and Peter, James, and John are located near the visitor's center. An older monument to the restoration of the Aaronic priesthood placed in 1960 is located closer to the river near to the Joseph and Emma Smith cabin.

On May 15, 1829, Joseph and Oliver came across a passage that struck them both. Joseph and Oliver went to the nearby by woods to inquire "respecting baptism for the remission of sins, that we found mentioned in the translation of the plates"(Joseph Smith-History 1:68). In answer to their prayer "a messenger from heaven descended in a cloud of light, and having laid his hands upon us" (Joseph-Smith History 1:68). The angel identified himself as the New Testament figure John the Baptist. The angel bestowed on Joseph and Oliver the priesthood of Aaron (see Doctrine and Covenants 13).

In a letter he wrote in 1834, Oliver provided his account of what led them to inquire about the authority to baptize: "After writing the account of the Savior's ministry to the remnant of the seed of Jacob, upon this continent, it was easily to be seen, as the prophet said would be, that darkness covered the earth and gross darkness the minds of the people. On reflecting further, it was easily to be seen, that amid the great strife and noise concerning religion, none had authority to administer in the name of Christ."[298] We do not know what passage Joseph and Oliver were translating when this question arose, though it is likely they were reading 3 Nephi 11:21–23, where the Savior bestows the authority to baptize on the Nephite disciples.

Oliver also offers a account of the angel's words than Joseph with small differences from Joseph's recollections. Oliver recorded the blessing from the angel as follows: "Upon you my fellow-servants, in the name of Messiah, I confer this Priesthood and this authority, which shall remain upon the earth, the Sons of Levi may yet offer an offering unto the Lord in righteousness!"[299] In his 1834 letter, Oliver refers only to "this Priesthood and this authority," though Joseph later specified that it was the "priesthood of Aaron" restored at this time (D&C 13). In later reminiscences, Oliver also specified that what John the Baptist restored was the Aaronic Priesthood.

The banks of the Susquehanna where the first baptisms took place and several angelic ministers appeared. Photo by Casey Paul Griffiths.

298 "Letter I," *Latter Day Saints' Messenger and Advocate*, October 1834, 1:13–16.
299 "Letter I," 1:13–16.

Oliver never wavered in his testimony of the experience with the angel, even during the years of 1838-1848, when he was no longer affiliated with the Church. In fact, in an 1846 letter, Oliver worried about how his character had been presented in the Church after his excommunication, writing, "I have been sensitive on this subject, I admit; but I ought to be so—you would be under the circumstances, had you stood in the presence of John, and with our departed brother Joseph, to receive the Lesser Priesthood."[300]

When Oliver returned to the Church in 1846, Reuben Miller recorded him sharing his testimony of these events in a public address to the Saints: "I was also present with Joseph when an holy angel from God came down from heaven and conferred on us, or restored, the lesser or Aaronic Priesthood, and said to us, at the same time, that it should remain upon the earth while the earth stands."[301] Samuel W. Richards was told by Oliver of the visit of "John the Baptist, holding the keys of the Aaronic Priesthood" and said that both the Aaronic and Melchizedek Priesthoods "with their authority, are now, and must continue to be in the body of the Church of Jesus Christ of Latter-day Saints."[302] Oliver Cowdery's account of these events, found in the scriptures at the end of Joseph Smith—History, in the Pearl of Great Price provides a second witness to Joseph's account of the manifestation of John the Baptist.

---

300 Letter to Phineas H. Young, March 23, 1846.

301 "Last Days of Oliver Cowdery," *Deseret News,* April 13, 1859.

302 See Larry E. Morris, *A Documentary History of the Book of Mormon,* 2019, 379.

The Appearance of Peter, James, and John

Monument honoring the appearance of Peter, James, and John. Photo by Casey Paul Griffiths.

Some historians have argued that the restoration of the Melchizedek Priesthood came in "the chamber of old Father Whitmer" (Doctrine and Covenants 128:21), and that Peter James and John later appeared to restore the keys of the apostleship.[303]

The keys bestowed by these ancient Apostles encompassed the power which was necessary to bring about the "dispensation of the fulness of times," which the Apostle Paul himself taught would "gather together in one all things in Christ, both which are in heaven, and which are on earth" (See Doctrine and Covenants 27:12-13; Ephesians 1:10). The Apostle Erastus Snow likewise taught, "This Priesthood conferred upon them by those three messengers embraces within it all offices of the Priesthood from the highest to the lowest. As has been often taught us that the keys of the presidency of this Apostleship represent the highest authority conferred upon man in the flesh. And by virtue of these keys of Priesthood the Prophet Joseph from time to time proceeded to ordain and set in order the Priesthood in its various quorums as we see it today in the Church."[304]

303 See Richard L. Bushman, *Joseph Smith: Rough Stone Rolling,* (New York: Alfred A. Knopf, 2005), 117-118.

304 *Journal of Discourses,* 23:183.

The First President and Twelve Apostles highlighted the importance of these angelic ministers when the Restoration Proclamation was issued in 2020, writing, "We affirm that under the direction of the Father and the Son, heavenly messengers came to instruct Joseph and re-establish the Church of Jesus Christ. The resurrected John the Baptist restored the authority to baptize by immersion for the remission of sins. Three of the original twelve Apostles—Peter, James, and John—restored the apostleship and keys of priesthood authority."[305]

The possibilities exist of even more angelic encounters along the banks of the Susquehanna. In his 1842 reminiscence, Joseph Smith wrote about "The voice of Michael on the banks of the Susquehanna, detecting the devil when he appeared as an angel of light!" (Doctrine and Covenants 128:20). The book of Revelations speaks of Michael casting Satan out of heaven (Revelation 12:7-9). We know nothing more about the confrontation between Michael and Satan than what is mentioned in Doctrine and Covenants 128, except that it took place somewhere near the Susquehanna. Joseph also wrote about "the voice of Michael, the archangel; the voice of Gabriel, and of Raphael, and of divers angels, from Michael or Adam down to the present time, all declaring their dispensation, their rights, their keys, their honors, their majesty and glory, and the power of their priesthood" (Doctrine and Covenants 128:21).

Mini-Devotional – "The Keys of the Ministering of Angels"

President David O. McKay once called the priesthood "our most distinguishing feature."[306] Another prophet, Gordon B. Hinckley, taught, ""[The priesthood] is a delegation of divine authority, different from all other powers and authorities on the face of the earth. … It is the only power on the earth that reaches beyond the veil of death. … Without it there could be a church in name only, [a church] lacking authority to administer in the things of God."[307] This divine authority allows men who hold the offices of the priesthood and women who hold priesthood authority to carry out God's work on the earth.

305 The Restoration of the Fulness of the Gospel of Jesus Christ, 2020.

306 Conference Report, April 1937, 21.

307 Gordon B. Hinckley, "Priesthood Restoration," *Ensign,* October 1988, 71.

- How has priesthood authority blessed your life?

The events that took place in Harmony represent the beginnings of the fulness of the priesthood returning to the earth after the apostasy. Other keys and authorities of the priesthood were restored in other places where the Church established roots. These ministering angels create a continuity from the time of Jesus Christ to the latter-days. Important powers such as "the keys of the ministering of angels" (Doctrine and Covenants 13).

- Angel is a Hebrew word that means "messenger." How have men and women today received the power to act as ministering angels?
- How have ministering angels blessed your life?

The Revelation to the Elect Lady

The rebuilt home of Isaac and Elizabeth Hale at the Priesthood Restoration site. Photo by Casey Paul Griffiths.

Several more revelations were received in Harmony, but among the most important is Doctrine and Covenants 25, given to Emma Smith in July 1830. Emma was baptized on June 28, 1830. However, before she was able to confirmed a member of the Church, Joseph Smith was caught up in an outbreak of persecution, dragged off to two different trials, and chased through the countryside by a mob. The opposition to the work in the regions around Emma's childhood home of Harmony, Pennsylvania, were increasing sharply. The trials exacted a high emotional toll on Emma. When Joseph's lawyer, John S. Reid, stopped by to check on Emma, he said that her face was "wet with tears . . . [and] her very heartstrings [were] broken with grief. In the midst of these difficulties, Joseph dictated this revelation on Emma's behalf.[308]

Most of the Doctrine and Covenants is simply addressed to all people, without any specifications about gender. At the same time, many of Joseph Smith's friends and family requested personal revelations addressed only to them. This is the only revelation in the Doctrine and Covenants given specifically to a woman. Because of its unique nature it has been spoken of as a revelation to all women in the Church.

President Gordon B. Hinckley applied this revelation to all women in the Church, declaring, "I remind you of a great and remarkable revelation given through the Prophet Joseph Smith to his wife Emma and applicable to every woman in the Church, for the Lord said in concluding this revelation 'that this is my voice unto all.' In the first verse of this revelation the Lord states that 'all those who receive my gospel are sons and daughters in my kingdom.' Great and true are these words of divine promise. The revelation which follows these opening words is rich in counsel, in praise, in instruction, and in promise to Emma Smith, and to every other woman who heeds the word of the Lord as set forth therein."[309]

Why did the Lord call Emma an "elect lady?" Twelve years after this revelation was given, at the first meeting of the Relief Society, Joseph Smith explained the meaning of this prophecy. According to the minutes of the Nauvoo Relief Society, "President Smith read the revelation to Emma Smith from the book of Doctrine and Covenants; and stated that she was ordained at the time, the revelation was given, to expound the scriptures to all; and to teach the female part of community."[310] Joseph Smith's journal records that he "gave much instruction, read in the New Testament, and Book of Doctrine and Covenants, concerning the Elect Lady, and showed that the elect meant to be elected to a certain work, and that the revelation was then fulfilled by Sister Emma's election to the Presidency of the

---

308 Newell and Avery, *Mormon Enigma: Emma Hale Smith,* 1984, 33–35).

309 "Daughters of God," October 1991 General Conference.

310 Nauvoo Relief Society Minute Book, 125, JSP.

Society, she having previously been ordained to expound the Scriptures."[311] Joseph also added "that not [Emma] alone, but others, may attain to the same blessings" found in this revelation.[312]

Representation of the gold plates. Emma Smith served as a scribe and testified that she moved the plates, but never saw them as other witnesses of the Book of Mormon did. Photo by Casey Paul Griffiths.

Emma served as one of the most important figures in the coming forth of the Book of Mormon. She acted as Joseph's scribe during the early stages of the translation. She served as a constant source of support to the prophet during the difficulties surrounding the lost manuscript. She believed whole-heartedly in the Book of Mormon for the rest of her life. In an interview with her son, Joseph III, she later commented, "My belief is that the Book of Mormon is of divine authenticity—I have not the slightest doubt of it. I am satisfied that no man could have dictated the writing of the manuscripts unless he was inspired; for, when acting as his scribe, your father would dictate to me hour after hour; and when returning after meals, or after interruptions, he could at once begin where he had left off, without either seeing the manuscript or having any portion of it read to him. This was a usual thing for him to do. It would have been improbable that a learned

311 JS Journal, Dec. 1841-Dec. 1842, 91, JSP.

312 Nauvoo RS Minute Book, 8, JSP).

man could do this; and, for one so ignorant and unlearned as he was, it was simply impossible."[313]

However, Emma was not chosen to be one of the witnesses of the Book of Mormon and did not see the plates. She later noted, "The plates often lay on the table without any attempt at concealment, wrapped in a small linen tablecloth, which I had given him to fold them in. I once felt of the plates, as they thus lay on the table, tracing their outline and shape. They seemed to be pliable like thick paper, and would rustle with a metallic sound when the edges were moved by the thumb, as one does sometimes thumb the edges of a book"[314]

The Lord's counsel for Emma to go with Joseph "at the time of his going" is most likely a reference to the growing tension with Emma's family over Joseph's prophetic calling. Emma's uncle, Nathaniel Lewis, was a Methodist minister and a leader of the persecutions that hindered Joseph during this time. Emma's father, Isaac Hale, was also antagonistic toward the work, later calling the Book of Mormon "a silly fabrication of falsehood and wickedness." In August 1833, a month after this revelation was given, Joseph and Emma left Harmony, Pennsylvania, because of persecution. Emma never saw her family again.[315]

Joseph Smith saw Emma as his constant companion through the travails of his prophetic ministry. Near the end of his life, he remarked, "With what unspeakable delight, and what transports of joy swelled my bosom, when I took by the hand on that night, my beloved Emma she that was my wife, even the wife of my youth; and the choice of my heart. Many were the re-vibrations of my mind when I contemplated for a moment the many scenes we had been called to pass through. The fatigues, and the toils, the sorrows, and sufferings, and the joys and consolations from time to time had strewed our paths and crowned our board. Oh! what a co-mingling of thought filled my mind for the moment, Again she is here, even in the seventh trouble, undaunted, firm and unwavering, unchangeable, affectionate Emma."[316]

---

313 "Last Testimony of Sister Emma," *Saint's Herald,* vol. 26, no. 19, 289).

314 "Last Testimony of Sister Emma," *Saint's Herald,* vol. 26, no. 19, 289.

315 *Documentary History of the Book of Mormon,* 2019, pp. 80–83).

316 Joseph Smith Journal, Dec. 1841-Dec. 1842, 164, JSP.

The grave of Joseph and Emma's first son is found in the cemetery next to the Priesthood Restoration site. Photo by Casey Paul Griffiths.

Mini-Devotional: "Daughters in My Kingdom"

The Savior saw Emma Smith's distress and offered words of affirmation and comfort to her. He also made the statement that "all those who receive my gospel are sons and daughters in my kingdom" (Doctrine and Covenants 25:1). This revelation became the charter for all women in the Church. It underlines their roles as teachers of the scripture and calls them to receive education and use their talents (Doctrine and Covenants 25:7-8,11). Take a minute to reflect on the importance of the role women play in the Church, beginning with Emma Smith down to the present.

- How have righteous women played a role in your life and your growth?
- Why is it important for all women to know that they are daughters of Heavenly Parents, and through righteous living can become daughters of Jesus Christ? (Doctrine and Covenants 25:1).

Significant events at this location:

- Joseph Smith was employed as a farmhand in 1826 by Joseph Knight Sr.
- Joseph Knight Sr. loaned Joseph Smith his sleigh to court Emma Hale.
- First miracle of the restored Church was performed by Joseph Smith in April 1830.
- Baptisms were performed on the Knight farm on June 28, 1830.
- Joseph Smith was arrested, arraigned, and acquitted twice in two days.
- The Colesville branch was organized.

THE KNIGHT FAMILY HOME IN COLESVILLE

The home of Joseph Sr. and Polly Knight in Colesville has been restored and hosts visitors from April to October every year. Photo by Casey Paul Griffiths.

Located in present day Nineveh, New York, the home of Joseph Knight Sr. was the home of many of the most stalwart Saints of the early Restoration and the site of several early miracles. The family of Joseph Knight Sr. formed the nucleus of the Colesville Branch of the Church, a group of Saints who played a central role in the saga of the Restoration. During the translation of the Book of Mormon and in the infancy of the Church, the support of the Knight family allowed Joseph Smith and his associates to complete their work. The Knights and the Saints in this area followed the work of the Restoration from Colesville through every phase of the work until they made their home in the Western United States.

The sites in this area are not operated by the site but are overseen by the Colesville Restoration, Inc. that employs their own docents for the sites. The sites in Colesville include the restored Joseph Knight Sr. home and the Josiah Stowell Home. Tour guides are usually at the home from the beginning of May through the end of October. It is best to call ahead before arriving at the sites to let them know you are coming. You can find the contact info at the website for Colesville Restoration Inc.[317]

Joseph Smith Comes to Colesville

The home of Josiah Stowell is located near to the Knight home and is also open for tours in the Summer months. Photo by Casey Paul Griffiths.

Hoping to discover a silver mine, Josiah Stowell hired Joseph Smith to dig for him in October 1825. During his employment, Joseph boarded at the home of Isaac Hale, where he first met his future wife, Emma Hale.

317 Contact information for the Colesvilles Restoration Inc. can be found at http://www.colesville-restoration.com/444952111, (accessing June 20, 2022). The phone number to contact the guides at the site is 607-595-0732. The site is usually open from 9am to 6pm from May to October.

After working for Josiah for a few months, the Prophet "prevailed with the old gentleman to cease digging after it [Spanish treasure]."[318]

About 3.5 miles southwest of Josiah Stowell's property lay a large farm of about 142 acres owned by a man named Joseph Knight Sr.[319] Joseph was a friend of Josiah, and because of the size of Joseph's farm, he often hired farm hands to help with daily labor. Josiah recommended Joseph Smith to Joseph Knight as a farm hand, and the young Prophet began working for Joseph in 1826. Newel K. Knight, Joseph Knight's son, later wrote in his journal: "The business in which my father was engaged often required him to have hired help, and among the many from time to time employed was a young man by the name of Joseph Smith, Jun., to whom I was particularly attached. His noble deportment, his faithfulness and his kind address, could not fail to win the esteem of those who had the pleasure of his acquaintance."[320]

Joseph Smith quickly developed a close friendship with members of the Knight family, a relationship that enabled him to trust them enough to share personal experiences with them, including the First Vision and the subsequent visits of the angel Moroni concerning the buried golden plates. Newel Knight related, "My father said Joseph was the best hand he ever hired, we found him a boy of truth, he was 21 years of age. I think it was in November [1826] he made known to my father and I, that he had seen a vision, that a personage had appeared to him and told him where there was a gold book of ancient date buried, and if he would follow the directions of the Angel, he could get it. We were told it in secret."[321] The Knights were supportive of Joseph and became not only some of his closest friends but also some of the first believers of the restored gospel.

While employed by the Knights in the winter of 1826, Joseph Smith began to take regular trips to Harmony, Pennsylvania, to visit Emma Hale. Joseph Knight Sr. lent Joseph Smith his horse and sleigh so he could travel more than thirty miles from the Knight farm in Colesville to Harmony to

318 Joseph Smith History, A-1, 8, JSP.

319 Larry C. Porter, "The Colesville Branch and the Coming Forth of the Book of Mormon," *BYU Studies Quarterly* 10, no. 3 (1970): 368.

320 Newel Knight, Autobiography and journal, circa 1846–1847, MS 767, Church History Library, Salt Lake City.

321 Joseph Knight Jr., "Joseph Knight's [Jr.] Incidents of History from 1827 to 1844," comp. Thomas Bullock, August 16, 1862, MS 286, Church History Library, Salt Lake City.

court Emma. He also lent his sleigh to Joseph on January 18, 1827, when Joseph and Emma eloped to be married.[322]

The following September, Joseph Smith was able to obtain the golden plates from the Hill Cumorah, once again using Joseph Knight's horse and wagon.[323] When Joseph Smith was attacked by three men who attempted to steal the plates from him, Joseph Knight was among those who pursued the assailants.

The Knights were also instrumental in supporting the translation process of the Book of Mormon. In the spring of 1829, Joseph found himself impoverished, having dedicated all his time to translation instead of paid labor. To help facilitate the divine work in which the Prophet was engaged, Joseph Knight brought food and writing supplies to Harmony so the translation could continue. He wrote, "I Bought a Barral of Mackrel and some lined paper for writing. And when I Came home I Bought some nine or ten Bushels of grain and five or six Bushels of taters and a pound of tea, and I went Down to see him and they ware in want. Joseph and Oliver ware gone to see if they Could find a place to work for provisions. But found none. They returned home and found me there with provisions, and they ware glad for they ware out."[324]

Mini-Devotional—The Value of Friendship

The Knights were true friends to the Prophet Joseph Smith. Joseph Smith many times relied on Joseph Knight Jr. and Newel Knight Jr. to be loyal, supportive friends. The Prophet Joseph Smith valued friendship and even declared, "Friendship is one of the grand fundamental principles of 'Mormonism'; [it is designed] to revolutionize and civilize the world and cause wars and contentions to cease and men to become friends and brothers."[325]

- How is friendship a grand fundamental of Mormonism?
- What made the Knights such good friends to the Prophet?

---

322 Dean C. Jessee, "Joseph Knight's Recollection of Early Mormon History," *BYU Studies Quarterly* 17, no. 1 (1976): 30.

323 Lucy Smith, *Biographical Sketches of Joseph Smith, the Prophet, and His Progenitors for Many Generations* (Liverpool, 1853), 99–101.

324 Jessee, "Joseph Knight's Recollection," 10.

325 "History, 1838–1856, volume E-1 [1 July 1843–30 April 1844]," p. 1680, JSP.

- Who are the friends in your life who have been there for you?
- What makes you a good friend?

The Knight Family Are Converted to the Gospel

Representations of Joseph Knight Sr. found in the Knight home. Photo by Casey Paul Griffiths.

After the publication of the Book of Mormon and the official organization of the Church in 1830, the Knight family farm in Colesville continued to be an important locale for early Latter-day Saints. In the same month that the Book of Mormon was published, the prophet Joseph Smith visited the Knight family in Colesville. Joseph identified the Knights as Universalists (Universalists believe that the entire human family will be saved), but they "were willing to reason with me upon my religious views and were as usual friendly and hospitable." One member of the family that seemed especially engaged in Joseph's work and teachings was Newel Knight. Joseph said that he and Newel "had many serious conversations on the important subject of man's eternal salvation." Newel was an active attendee at the church meetings Joseph held while staying in the Colesville township.[326]

326 Joseph Smith History, A-1, 39–40, JSP.

The First Miracle of the Restored Church of Jesus Christ of Latter-day Saints

While the Prophet was staying at the Knight family farm, the first miracle of the restored Church was performed, and Newel Knight was the recipient. Newel had refused an invitation to pray vocally at one of the church gatherings. Later, he retired to the woods near the Knight farm to pray privately in an attempt to prepare himself to do so publicly if he was asked again. While attempting to pray in the woods, he was overcome by an evil spirit which distorted and twisted his limbs. When he returned home, his alarmed wife, Sally, sent for Joseph Smith. In Joseph's words, "I went and found him suffering very much in his mind, and his body acted upon in a very strange manner; his visage and limbs distorted and twisted in every shape and appearance possible to imagine; and finally, he was caught up off the floor of the apartment and tossed about most fearfully."

Upon feeling Joseph Smith grab his hand, Newel Knight asked him to cast out the demon that was inside him, expressing faith in Joseph's ability to do so. Joseph replied, "If you know that I can, it shall be done." The Prophet then reported, "I rebuked the devil, and commanded him in the name of Jesus Christ to depart from him; when immediately Newel spoke out and said that he saw the devil leave him and vanish from his sight. This was the first miracle which was done in the Church, or by any member of it. . . . It was done by God, and by the power of godliness." Of the small crowd of friends, neighbors, and family members who had witnessed this scene, the majority were later baptized as members of the Church. Newel subsequently visited Joseph in Fayette, New York and was baptized by David Whitmer the last week of May that same year.[327]

Baptisms Performed on the Knight Farm on June 28, 1830

Despite the hospitality shown to the Prophet by the Knight family in Colesville, others were not as welcoming. Joseph Smith, accompanied by Oliver Cowdery and John and David Whitmer, visited Colesville again in June 1830, and local opposition to Joseph and his teachings became hostile.

327 Joseph Smith History, A-1, 40–41, The Joseph Smith Papers, JSP.

Upon arriving in the Colesville township, the Prophet found a group ready to be baptized into the Church. They had built a dam in the nearby river to perform the baptisms the next day. That Saturday night, a local mob (later found to have been assembled by preachers in the area) gathered and destroyed the dam.

That next Monday morning, Joseph Smith and others quickly constructed another dam in order to perform the baptisms before the mob could reassemble. Thirteen people were baptized, including Emma Smith and three members of the Knight family: Joseph Sr., Joseph Jr., and Polly. The mob, enraged that the baptisms had been performed, surrounded the Knight family farm and threatened violence.

The Arrest and Arraignment of Joseph Smith

Artifacts found during the restoration of the Knight family home. Photo by Casey Paul Griffiths.

While preparing to confirm the newly baptized members, the town constable visited the Knight farm with a warrant for Joseph Smith's arrest on charges of disorderly conduct. Soon after the arrest, the constable informed Joseph that he had conspired with the mob to lead Joseph into an ambush, but having "found [him] to be a different person than that which was represented to him," he "was determined to save [Joseph] from them."[328] Joseph recorded, "I soon found that he had told me the truth in this matter, for not far from Mr. Knight's house, the wagon in which we had set out was surrounded by a mob, who seemed only to await some signal from the constable; but to their great disappointment, he gave the horse the whip, and drove me out of their reach." The mob set out in close pursuit of Joseph and the constable, nearly catching them when they had to replace a broken wheel on the wagon, but the two men ultimately arrived safely at the town of South Bainbridge in Chenango County. At their lodgings for the night, the constable even slept on the floor with his boots to the door in order to protect Joseph from harm.

Amidst this chaos caused by the mob's threats and Joseph Smith's arrest, Joseph Knight obtained the help of two of his neighbors to come to the aid of the incarcerated Prophet. James Davidson and John Reid were "respectable farmers, men renowned for their integrity, and well versed in the laws of their country." The day following the Prophet's arrest, a trial was held, and witnesses were called upon to testify. Among these first witnesses were Josiah Stowell and his daughters and a man named Jonathan Thompson, from whom Joseph Smith had bought a yoke of oxen. The witnesses all testified in favor of Joseph, affirming the stalwart nature of his character and the virtue of his actions both in public and in private. Realizing that Joseph would be promptly acquitted of the charges, enemies of the prophet obtained a warrant for Joseph's arrest out of a neighboring county, and he was arrested once again immediately following the close of the day's trial.[329]

The constable that arrested Joseph Smith and took him to Broome County was not nearly as amiable as the one from Bainbridge, and Joseph's requests to return home to spend the night with his wife were denied. The Prophet wrote:

> The constable . . . had no sooner arrested me than he began to abuse and insult me; and so unfeeling was he with me, that although I had been kept all day in court without anything to eat since the morning, yet he hurried me off to Broome County, a distance of about fifteen miles, before he allowed me any kind of food whatever. He took me to a tavern, and gathered in a number of men, who used every means to abuse, ridicule and insult me. They spit upon me, pointed their fingers at me,

328 Joseph Smith History, A-1, 42–44, JSP.
329 Joseph Smith History, A-1, 44–45, JSP.

> saying, "Prophesy, prophesy!" and thus did they imitate those who crucified the Savior of mankind, not knowing what they did.[330]

The following day, another trial was held for the Prophet. Joseph Knight once again implored his neighbors for legal help, and although they were weary from the proceedings of the previous day, they agreed to represent Joseph Smith once again. As with the first trial, witnesses were called upon to testify against Joseph. These witnesses, Joseph said, "swore to the most palpable falsehoods,"[331] and their stories were so full of contradictions that their testimonies could not be admitted.

Eventually, Newel Knight was called to the stand and was questioned by Mr. Seymour, a lawyer for the prosecution, who asked about his experience of having the devil cast out of him by the Prophet. Newel testified that the miracle was done by the power of God through Joseph Smith. Attempting to impeach Newel, Seymour asked him what the devil looked like as it left his body. Newel expressed a willingness to answer but first asked the lawyer if he understood the things of the spirit. When the lawyer replied in the negative, Newel chose not to describe the devil, for "it was a spiritual sight, and spiritually discerned," and the lawyer "would not understand it were [he] to tell [him] of it."[332]

After the final statements, which appear to have mostly centered on the character of Joseph Smith, the trial was concluded, and the prophet was acquitted once again. The constable who had treated Joseph poorly the night before asked Joseph for forgiveness. He then informed Joseph of yet another ploy by the mob to subject him to rail-riding and tarring and feathering if he was acquitted, but the constable was willing to escort Joseph out safely through a private path.[333]

A few days after the second trial, Joseph Smith and Oliver Cowdery returned to the Knight family farm to confirm the recently baptized Colesville Latter-day Saints. They had scarcely arrived at the Knight's property when a mob was once again assembled. Joseph and Oliver fled from the mob and traveled through the night to arrive safely home. The Colesville members were successfully confirmed members of the Church later that year.

---

330 Joseph Smith History, A-1, 44–45, JSP.

331 "History, circa June 1839–circa 1841 [Draft 2]," p. 46, JSP.

332 "History, circa 1841, draft [Draft 3]," p. 79, JSP.

333 Joseph Smith History, A-1, 46–47, JSP.

Mini-Devotional—Knowledge of Joseph Smith's Character

We know of the experiences that Joseph Smith underwent as well as the actions of Joseph and others during the trials through the historical records, which enable us to better understand the true nature of Joseph's character. Ever since Joseph's vision of the Father and Son, the adversary has worked to discredit his character. The two constables slandered the Prophet by design of the mobs, and both had individually conspired with mobs to harm Joseph. However, after meeting the Prophet, their eyes were opened, and both helped Joseph even though they put their own lives in danger for doing so.

Many people today have questions regarding Joseph Smith. The adversary works just as efficiently now as he did two hundred years ago to spread lies and misinformation against the Prophet of the Restoration, and, just like the two constables, many are led astray into believing that Joseph was not who he claimed to be.

The Lord gave us the way to determine the true character of men who claim to be called of God: "A good tree cannot bring forth evil fruit, neither can a corrupt tree bring forth good fruit. . . . Wherefore by their fruits ye shall know them" (Matt. 7:18).

- What good fruit has Joseph brough forth?
- How does the good fruit that Joseph brought forth testify of his good character?

The Colesville Branch

List of the original members of the Colesville branch at the Knight family home. Photo by Casey Paul Griffiths.

Latter-day Saints living around the Colesville township became numerous enough to form a branch. The Colesville branch was first presided over by Hyrum Smith, who soon passed the responsibility on to Newel Knight.[334] In December 1830, Joseph received a revelation that instructed the Latter-day Saints to gather in Ohio (Doctrine and Covenants 37). The Colesville branch faithfully responded to the Lord's call despite significant financial difficulties, and under Newel's leadership, they began their trek to Kirtland in April 1831.

Despite being recent converts, the Knights trusted implicitly in the prophetic calling of their friend Joseph Smith. Newel Knight later wrote: "As might be expected, we were obliged to make great sacrifices of our property. The most of my time was occupied in visiting the brethren, and helping to arrange their affairs, so that we might travel together in one company. Having made the best arrangements, we could for the journey, we bade adieu to all we held dear on this earth and . . . started for our destination."[335] The Colesville branch was the first group of Latter-day Saints to follow the Prophet to Kirtland.[336]

334 Porter, "Colesville Branch," 368.

335 Newel Knight Jr., "Newel Knight's Journal," in *Scraps of Biography*, ed. Juvenile Instructor Office (Salt Lake City, 1883), 68–69.

336 Stanley B. Kimball, "The First Road West: From New York to Kirtland, 1831," *Ensign*, January 1979.

The Knights and other Colesville members stand as a testament of the power of faith that accompanies true conversion. When they moved to Kirtland, the Knights had known Joseph Smith for only five years and had been baptized members of the Church for less than one year. Joseph's name had been slandered repeatedly, and many enemies of the Church sought to cause him harm. Despite all of this, the Colesville Saints were willing to sell all that they owned and leave all that they had known in order to heed the call of a man who they knew to be a true prophet of God.

EPILOGUE

Why Did the Saints Leave New England?

Apple trees and the Smith family farm. Photo by Casey Paul Griffiths.

Unlike other places where the Church established its headquarters, the Saints didn't leave New England because they were driven out. While it is true that the Saints in New York and Pennsylvania faced persecution they did not leave their homes and farms because of threats against their lives. They left because of a commandment from the Lord, given to them in December 1831. This revelation, one of the shortest in the entire Doctrine and Covenants, simply commanded "a commandment I give unto the church, that it is expedient in me that they should assemble together at the Ohio" (Doctrine and Covenants 37:3). The Saints left New England because the Lord commanded them; because of their faith in the revelations given to their Prophet.

This gathering was the first in a series of gatherings carried out during the 19th century and continuing into our time. This practice of gathering led the Saints to new homes in Ohio, Missouri, Illinois and other places. Eventually it culminated int the epic story of an entire people who departed into the wilderness of the American West to found a inland commonwealth of hundreds of settlements. At the same time converts from around the globe gathering to build a cities and temples in the mountains of North America. Eventually other temples were built until today every continent except Antarctica houses communities and temples built by the Saints. But the first step of this global gathering – a movement that spanned whole continents – began when the New England Saints took their first steps toward the West.

A second revelation on the gathering clarified some of the reasons for the Saints to leave their homes behind in New England. The revelation clarified that command to gather came "that ye might escape the power of the enemy, and be gathered unto me a righteous people, without spot and blameless" (Doctrine and Covenants 38:31). The Lord also promised them that Saints obeyed his command to gather "I will give unto you my law; and there you shall be endowed with power from on high" (Doctrine and Covenants 38:32). With this promise, the Saints followed counsel and gave up their homes and livelihoods in New England to gather to the Ohio.

The drama of the unfolding Restoration can be traced in the stories of the years following these families. The Smith family, the heart of the Palmyra branch of the Church, gathered and settled primarily in and around Kirtland, Ohio. They lived there in relative peace for nearly six years, helping to build the first temple and serving in various Church positions. Joseph Smith Sr. was called as the first Church patriarch in this dispensation, while William Smith was called as one of the original Twelve Apostles of this dispensation. Joseph Smith's other brothers and sisters formed a core system of support around him during the Ohio period. They lived in Kirtland until a financial crisis caused the collapse of the Church there. Fleeing to Missouri they found even worse persecutions awaiting them. They endured the travails of Missouri, fleeing as refugees to Illinois where they found refuge in a swampy peninsula, drained and rebuilt as the city of Nauvoo. In Nauvoo the Smiths remained core supporters of Joseph's prophetic mission, with Hyrum Smith being elevated to the position of Assistant President of the Church (see Doctrine and Covenants 124:91-94).

Nauvoo was also a time of loss for the Smith family. Their beloved patriarch, Joseph Sr., died in 1840. Don Carlos, the Prophet's younger brother, passed in 1841. An infant child of Joseph and Emma, named in honor of Don Carlos, died just a week later. The tragic events of the summer of 1844 took the lives of Joseph, Hyrum and Samuel Smith. William Smith, the last surviving Smith son, was excommunicated in October 1845 when he tried to wrest control of the Church from the Twelve Apostles. When the main body of the Church departed from Nauvoo, Lucy Mack, Sophronia, Katherine, and Lucy Smith all remained behind, living near Nauvoo for the rest of their lives.

The branch of the Church in Fayette centered around the family of Peter and Mary Musselman Whitmer. The Whitmers left behind their farm, the first headquarters of the Church, and moved first to Kirtland and then to Missouri to assist in building the promised Zion. They remained faithful through the terrible persecutions that forced the Saints from their homes in Jackson County, Missouri in the 1833. The Whitmer remained as pillars of the Church in Missouri, but the persecutions took their toll on them physically. Christian and Peter Whitmer Jr. died in 1835 and 1836 respectively, while the Saints were still refugees in Clay County, Missouri. The rest of the Whitmer family came into conflict with Joseph Smith and other Church leaders during a financial crisis in Kirtland in 1837. David and John Whitmer, both witnesses of the Book of Mormon, were excommunicated in the Spring of 1838. The rest of the Whitmer family became disaffected from the Church and left. Most of the Whitmer settled in Richmond, Missouri, and remained there for the rest of their lives.

The family of Joseph and Polly Knight, the heart of the Colesville branch of the Church, also obeyed the commandment to gather to Ohio in 1831. They arrived and were welcomed to settle on lands consecrated to the Church by Leman Copley, an Ohio convert to the Church from the nearby sect of Shakers. Unfortunately, Copley broke his covenant to live the law of consecration, forcing the Knights to leave Ohio and travel onward to new homes in Missouri (see Doctrine and Covenants 54). The Knights moved on to Missouri, even though Polly Knight was gravely ill. She was able to see the promised land of Zion before she died a few days later. The

Prophet Joseph Smith, who traveled to Missouri around the same time as the Knights, presided at the funeral.

The Knights were forced to leave their homes during the 1833 Missouri persecutions and again during the persecutions of 1838. They settled in Nauvoo and remained close friends with Joseph and Emma. When Brigham Young and the Twelve led the exodus from Nauvoo the Knights followed them. The journey to the West took a toll on the Knight family. Joseph Knight Sr., the family patriarch, passed away in 1847 at Mount Pisgah, Iowa. Newell Knight, the eldest son and leader of the family, passed away the same year in Nebraska. But the Knights pressed onward, with most of them settling in Utah and remaining faithful to the Church. One of their descendants, Jesse Knight, became a wealthy mining magnate and played a significant role in helping the Church and its educational institutions prosper.

Until the early 20th Century, the Church had virtually no presence in the New England states. These sacred lands—the cradle of the Restoration—were no longer home to those who believed in the Restoration of the Gospel of Jesus Christ in the latter days. This began to change when Willard and Rebecca Bean were called on a mission to the Palmyra area in 1915. The Beans took care of the Church properties newly purchased in and around Palmyra. They worked to heal old conflicts with the local people who still held animosity toward the Church. Willard, a former middleweight boxer, even held exhibition boxing matches to drum up publicity for the Church. They remained in the area until 1939 when they returned to Salt Lake City. By the time they left there were three growing branches of the Church.

Today New England is home to thousands of Latter-day Saints. Temples dot the landscape from the Palmyra temple, not far from the Sacred Grove, to the Boston, Massachusetts temple, near the earliest scenes of the American revolution. New England is still the cradle of the Restoration, but it is also a place where the grand saga of The Church of Jesus Christ of Latter-day Saints is being acted out every day in the lives of all those who hear the voice of God.

ABOUT THE AUTHORS

Casey Paul Griffiths is an Associate Professor of Church History and Doctrine at Brigham Young University. He holds a Bachelors, Masters, and PhD degrees from Brigham Young University. He is the author of numerous books and articles on the history of the Church including 50 Relics of the Restoration. He serves in leadership positions in numerous historical and educational associations, including the John Whitmer Historical Association. He is one of the managing editors of Doctrine and Covenants Central. He enjoys giving tours to Church History Sites and the Holy Land. He lives in Saratoga Springs with his wife Elizabeth and their four children.

Mary Jane Woodger, Ed.D., is a professor of Church history and doctrine at Brigham Young University. She completed her master of education degree at Utah State University, and received from Brigham Young University a doctor of education degree in educational leadership, with a minor in Church history and doctrine. Dr. Woodger has written and published over a dozen books, including three about the life and teachings of David O. McKay. She has also authored numerous articles on doctrinal, historical, and educational subjects. These articles have appeared in various academic journals, as well as the Journal of Book of Mormon Studies, the Church News, the Ensign, and The Religious Educator. Dr. Woodger has received several awards for her teaching and writing.